With love to

Nelda

We become our heroes
our mentors
those we admire most

Joe

Joe L - Wheeler
Conifer, Colorado

EVERYDAY
HEROES

EVERYDAY
HEROES

INSPIRING STORIES *of*
ORDINARY PEOPLE WHO MADE
A DIFFERENCE

COMPILED & EDITED BY

JOE WHEELER

WATERBROOK
PRESS

EVERYDAY HEROES
PUBLISHED BY WATERBROOK PRESS
2375 Telstar Drive, Suite 160
Colorado Springs, Colorado 80920
A division of Random House, Inc.

Woodcut illustrations are from the library of Joe Wheeler.

ISBN 1-57856-322-4

Published in association with the literary agency of Alive Communications, Inc.,
7680 Goddard Street, Suite 200, Colorado Springs, CO 80920.

Printed in the United States of America
2002—First Edition

10 9 8 7 6 5 4 3 2 1

There is one profession that is, all too often, both unsung and underappreciated. And many in the profession are unpaid, as they are volunteers. Daily they risk their lives on our behalf.

So it is that I dedicate this collection of hero stories to our nation's heroic firefighters. More specifically, because September 11, 2001, represents perhaps the greatest loss of firefighters in our history (343 in all), I dedicate this book to those who died in the collapse of the twin towers of the World Trade Center:

THE BRAVE FIREFIGHTERS
OF NEW YORK CITY

CONTENTS

Publisher's Note

Prepare yourself for a treat in this collection: Dr. Joe Wheeler quite likely knows more about a period he calls "the Golden Age of Judeo-Christian stories" (1870s–1950s) than any other person alive today. Two lifetimes have gone into this priceless collection: his mother's and his own. During that time period, traditional family values were incorporated into stories by virtually every family or children's magazine in America and, in the process, certain authors became cherished and honored everywhere. The best of these stories are cathartic: almost impossible to read without laughter and tears. Occasionally the language and punctuation may seem archaic to the modern-day reader, but Dr. Wheeler has tried to preserve these stories as they were originally written, convinced that to contemporize them would be to destroy their original beauty and power.

The illustrations in this volume also provide a special treat for the reader. The original editors of Dr. Wheeler's now best-selling Christmas in My Heart series wanted to choose a type of illustration that would be as timeless as the stories themselves. They concluded that only the woodcut illustrations from Dr. Wheeler's personal collection, which dates back hundreds of years, would be that timeless. Immediately the readers voted with their dollars that they loved this nostalgic return to the past, and they have insisted that he continue illustrating subsequent story collections with such "old-timey" illustrations. As a result, Dr. Wheeler has scoured America and England for century-old (or older) illustrations.

So when a new volume such as *Everyday Heroes* reaches the illustration stage, what happens? Let's ask the anthologizer himself.

Well, considering the fact that rarely do any of these old-time stories come with their own illustrations, there are no easy answers or quick fixes. I first have to graph out every story line in the book, which takes considerable time. Then I turn pages in old books and magazines ten to fifteen hours a day for four to six weeks, searching for an illustration that jumps out at me, that perfectly matches one of the story lines as well as my mental picture of what the characters look like. Before I'm done I will have pored through well over one hundred thousand pages just to find illustrations for fifteen to twenty-three stories. But that solid month and a half will be worth it all if those illustrations enhance the stories and bring joy to my readers. Even more worth it, if readers write to tell me how much the stories and illustrations mean to them.

It is with delight that we take you back in time with this collection of wonderful stories—human-interest narratives that model the courage and commitment to do what is right in a world gone wrong. We do so with the hope that such everyday heroism might be rekindled for a new era—that we, our children, and our children's children will determine once again to embrace virtue and honor as a way of life, as did many of our predecessors.

Since most of the stories were written decades ago, you may find occasional terminology or punctuation not common today—even word usage that, while not used derogatorily, might be considered "politically incorrect" in modern times. With the exception of only occasional, minor alterations, the editor and publisher have deliberately chosen to leave the stories as they were written in order to preserve the tone and voice of their day. As you read, however, please do take into consideration the social mores of the times in which the authors wrote.

EVERYDAY
HEROES

ON THE TRAIL
OF A HERO

Joseph Leininger Wheeler

We do indeed become our heroes, our mentors, those we admire most. Once our pantheon of heroes included the likes of Joseph, David, Daniel, Moses, Samuel, and Paul in Scripture; Davy Crockett, Daniel Boone, Kit Carson, Johnny Appleseed, and Buffalo Bill in legend; and George Washington, Thomas Jefferson, Abraham Lincoln, and Teddy and Franklin Roosevelt among our presidents.

In recent years these heroes had been replaced by new icons: faces we see on the screen every day—television actors, cinema actors, MTV performers, baseball players, football players, basketball players, hockey players, golfers, television hosts, sitcom celebrities, and even those who make it big in advertisements. The meringue displaced the filling, the hype displaced the substance, the illusion displaced the real.

I am reminded of the game of crack the whip we used to play when young. As ice skaters, each holding the hand of another, we'd skate faster and faster; not so fast if you were close to the hub, faster if you were farther out, until eventually gravity and centrifugal force would fling you away and splay you over the ice. The pace of our lives seems to me much like that old game we used to play. Every year we skate faster, until life seems almost a blur. We go faster and faster and faster, yet we no longer know where we've been, where we are, or where we're going. We get up early in the morning, turn on the news, dress and eat on the run, dress and feed the kids on the run, propel the kids to the bus or the school, race for the office, work all day (connected like octopuses to computers, fax machines, e-mail, telephones, television monitors, radio, mail, and real people), race home, get the kids into their chores and homework, get dinner ready, and eat with the television blaring. Then one spouse runs off for a second job, leaving the other to keep the lid on things until bedtime, when one by one each member of the family falls asleep. The next day it happens all over again.

In this crack-the-whip world in which we live, have we had the guts to emancipate ourselves from the frenzied whirl, take off our skates, find our way to a quiet spot, sit down, and ponder the Three Eternal Questions of life: *Who am I? Where have I come from? Where am I going?* Only when we have the courage to do this will we realize that we've been following pseudoheroes rather than real ones, and that we've been programming our children to do the same thing. It is usually not until we have contemplated our lives and communed with God that we take the next step: a careful scrutiny of the "heroes" we've been blindly following.

All of that changed, suddenly, in the nightmare of September 11, 2001, when fanatical terrorists commandeered four U.S. passenger airliners and crashed two into the Twin Towers of New York's World Trade Center, one into the Pentagon, and another into a field in Pennsylvania. As Americans stared at their television sets in surreal horror, tens of thousands of individuals in New York

City, Washington, D.C., Pennsylvania, and across the nation stepped forward to help in any way they could. Over four hundred New York police and firefighters who had entered the Twin Towers to rescue office workers lost their own lives when the towers fell. Thousands of professionals along with hundreds of search-and-rescue volunteers put their lives on the line to search for survivors. In the aftermath of the tragedy, hundreds of heartrending stories emerged from the wreckage and rubble—of individuals who risked their lives to lead others to safety, of airphone operators who calmed frightened passengers, of passengers who determined to take back their hijacked airliner—a move that cost them their lives but most likely saved hundreds of lives on the ground.

We have found new heroes in our midst. Not the glamorous or the famous, but the everyday heroes. Ordinary people like you and me. Men, women, and children who rose to the challenge amid extraordinary circumstances.

Never will I forget an older student who was in one of my freshman composition classes. As part of an assignment that came to be known as the "Nightingale assignment," I had mandated an hour's silence each day. Many, if not most, college freshmen could not remember the last time they had experienced this much silence, and at first they didn't know what to do with it. They didn't know how to talk to themselves. They didn't even know who they were, in fact. Well, this wife and mother in my class was no different. The silence staggered her. So did our later follow-up class discussions about our heroes—who or what might be the driving force in each of our lives. This mother-wife actually got angry with me for even suggesting that she might not know who her mentors or heroes might be. In fact, she stormed out of the classroom. That was on a Friday.

The following Monday afternoon is seared for all time in my

memory. This woman's face was the most serious I had ever seen it. Her hand waving in the air demanded attention. As close as I can remember it, she spoke to me first, apologizing for the vitriol she had spewed on me in the previous class; then she turned to the students and told them in almost solemn tones that she had a story to tell. There was almost absolute silence in that classroom as she said that for the first time since she could remember, she had unplugged her ears and unblinded her eyes. "I decided to pretend I was each of my children, and I watched television pretending I was seeing and listening as a three-year-old, a six-year-old, an eleven-year-old. I was appalled! I couldn't believe it! Where had I been all those years?"

For the first time she had *really* listened to the gutter talk in the talk shows, all the sexual double and triple entendres, the ridicule of God and Christians and decency, the advertisements that were blatantly at odds with the values and behavior she'd been trying to instill in her children. What she saw and heard on soaps and sitcoms almost curled her hair. She *really* listened to the lyrics on MTV, the radio, and the CDs her children were addicted to. She *really* watched and listened to the computer games her children played. We sat there in a kind of shock as she continued, often slowing to wipe away a tear or regain her composure. I'll venture to say that none of the freshmen who sat there spellbound that day will forget the experience.

For her and for them, for perhaps the first time in their lives, each began taking a serious look at whatever or whoever represented their central guiding force—their mentors, their heroes. They'd look at a baseball hero they idolized, yet his personal life was a shambles (with long strings of one-night stands); they'd look at a favorite football player and note his cheap shots and obscenities whenever he spoke; they'd look at a much-hyped Olympic gold medalist and remember her incredibly unsportsmanlike behavior; they'd look at the adored actor or actress, then take a hard look at the openly deviant lifestyle professed or the list of serial mates.

For a number of them, the upshot of this quiet time and the inner serenity was that they began searching for heroes they could respect. Some even searched out the ultimate hero of all—God.

THE NIGHTINGALE

Remember that the project was called the "Nightingale assignment"? Well, that name came from one of the most memorable—and true—stories that frontier writer Zane Grey ever wrote: "Monty Price's Nightingale." Monty was a cowboy who rode the Mogollon Rim country of northern Arizona about a hundred years ago. He had one driving force in his life that was so powerful nothing could stand in its way. Perhaps it was some form of dissipation; we are never told what. But there came a day when an equally powerful force came into his life: a little girl he dearly loved. For the first time in his life, the driving force (his nightingale) had a rival.

By the end of the freshman comp assignment (usually six weeks), each student also realized that one's nightingale was in all likelihood neither more nor less than one's heroes. Then the inevitable follow-up: Are these "heroes" the kind upon which they could safely construct their lives?

The subject of heroes has long fascinated me. Perhaps that's one reason I wrote my doctoral dissertation on Zane Grey, the Old West, and the fictional heroes Grey created. And it is a key reason why this book came to be. Because, deep down, I myself wanted to find out what the difference was between a genuine hero and a bogus one. The long journey to that knowledge has led me through hundreds of stories to those chosen for this collection. Each of my story finalists has helped to clarify in my mind what it really means to be a hero.

WEBSTER, HOUGHTON MIFFLIN, AND RANDOM HOUSE WEIGH IN

When asked by WaterBrook to put together a collection of stories about heroes, I deliberately delayed studying dictionary definitions of the word until I had put together the collection of stories, assuming that as I read them I'd gradually learn what these qualities were without even looking in the dictionary. Oh, I already thought I knew what a true hero was, but I wanted to see if my suppositions were correct.

At the end, I put these suppositions on trial with three great dictionaries: *Merriam-Webster's Collegiate Dictionary* (9th edition), Houghton Mifflin's *American Heritage Dictionary of the English Language,* and the renowned *Random House Webster's Unabridged Dictionary.* What I found in their pages meshed perfectly with the stories I had selected, but not in the least with today's popular use of the words *hero, heroine, heroic,* and *heroism.*

Surprisingly, I found little disagreement among these editors about what it meant to be a real hero. Certain defining words appeared in definition after definition. *Courage* was one of them. Clearly it is almost impossible to be a true hero without being courageous. A synonym, *daring,* was used as well, but more guardedly because *daring* comes with negative baggage that *courage* does not have.

Another word surfaced so often that I finally had to consider it an almost exact synonym: *noble,* a term used often in times past but so very little today. *Merriam-Webster's* editors declared that for one to be noble presupposed that one was superior in mind, character, ideals, and morals. Houghton Mifflin editors maintained that such a person would be lofty and exalted in character and would be characterized as great and magnanimous. Random House editors concurred, declaring that to be noble meant that one possessed an exalted moral character, that one was honorable, high-minded, and magnanimous; that one would scorn to be petty, mean, base, or dishonorable in any way; that one had greatness of mind and soul, especially as manifested in generosity and in overlooking injuries.

I also discovered that the word *heroic* in essence has no gender to it: the qualities apply equally to both sexes. To be heroic means that one's conduct has a high purpose to it, and that the desired results of that conduct are noble ones.

Nevertheless there is no question but that the word *hero* is more often associated with men than with women, with antecedents all the way back to myth and legend, to larger-than-life warriors of great strength and prowess who were known for their bold exploits. The antonym tells us a lot too: It is, quite simply, the word *coward.*

Characteristics of true heroes and heroines that few of us associate with the word include the following: one who is admired as a model or ideal, one who is characterized by godlike beneficence (doing good, being kind, practicing charity), one who is altruistic, one who is determined and intense, and one who is willing to risk, or even sacrifice, his or her life for another.

Judged by these criteria, few of our sports or Olympic stars would deserve to be called "heroes." As a matter of fact, in the aftermath of September 11, 2001, when we saw everyday people such as firefighters, police officers, search-and-rescue teams, and countless volunteers putting their personal safety and comfort on the line to help others, we are almost forced to come up with a new definition of a hero or a heroine. For the purposes of this study, I offer the following synthesis:

HERO. Someone worthy of admiration and emulation. An otherwise ordinary man, woman, or child who does extraordinary things. One who is noble (superior in mind, character, ideals, morals). One who places the good of others above self; in fact, is even willing to risk or even sacrifice his or her life for another, even were that person a stranger. One who has an unshakable sense of honor, whose integrity is as solid as the everlasting hills. One who is quietly self-assured—never ostentatious, proud, noblesse oblige, or demanding. One who is invariably kind and considerate of others—never meanspirited or vindictive. One who is generous and magnanimous, willing to forgive not only slights but terrible acts most others would consider unforgivable. One whose love embraces not only mankind but all of God's creatures. One who is courageous, daring, and bold. One who is so trustworthy you'd entrust everything you own—your life itself—to that person's keeping. One who is consistent, steadfast, dependable, and enduring: once a task or act is begun it is completed, no matter how difficult, no matter how many obstacles stand in the way, no matter how long the road. One who makes the world a better place than it would have been had he or she not lived.

There are two levels of heroism. The first, and by far the easiest to achieve, is the sudden act and the split-second decision that precipitates the act (an act that may be totally out of character with the rest of the person's life). The second, and by far the most difficult to achieve, is the heroic life; not merely a single act but a lifelong succession of moment-by-moment acts that are consistently heroic as I have already defined the word. It is this level of heroism the ancients would have ascribed to a demigod.

A hero, according to this definition, could also be defined as a living embodiment of Paul's ideal in 1 Corinthians 13 and, more recently, in Rudyard Kipling's great poem, "If":

> If you can keep your head when all about you
>   Are losing theirs and blaming it on you;
> If you can trust yourself when all men doubt you,
>   But make allowance for their doubting too;
> If you can wait and not be tired by waiting,
>   Or being lied about, don't deal in lies,
> Or being hated don't give way to hating,
>   And yet don't look too good, nor talk
>   too wise;

> If you can dream—and not make dreams your master;
>   If you can think—and not make thoughts
>   your aim,
> If you can meet with Triumph and Disaster
>   And treat those two imposters just the same;
> If you can bear to hear the truth you've spoken
>   Twisted by knaves to make a trap for fools,
> Or watch the things you gave your life to, broken,
>   And stoop and build 'em up with worn-out
>   tools;

If you can make one heap of all your winnings
    And risk it on one turn of pitch-and-toss,
And lose, and start again at your beginnings,
    And never breathe a word about your loss;
If you can force your heart and nerve and sinew
    To serve your turn long after they are gone,
And so hold on when there's nothing in you
    Except the Will which says to them:
        "Hold on!"

If you can talk with crowds and keep your virtue,
    Or walk with Kings—nor lose the common
        touch,
If neither foes nor loving friends can hurt you,
    If all men count with you, but none too much.
If you can fill the unforgiving minute
    With sixty seconds worth of distance run,
Yours is the Earth and everything that's in it,
    And—which is more—will you not hear:
    "Well done, My daughter…
    "Well done, My son."
                —Rudyard Kipling,
                1865–1936 (rephrased)

(I had the audacity to rephrase Kipling's last three lines above. I *had* to, because of a promise I made. I had just shared the poem in class, and a coed stayed afterward to express her tearful outrage at being excluded because of her gender [the original is addressed only to males]. To dry her tears, I promised to never again share the poem without a revised ending that would include the other half of the human race.)

As I look back through the year it has taken to pull this collection together, I realize that I had always assumed that heroism was reserved for the very few. I no longer believe that to be true. As we have now redefined heroism, it is clear to me that heroism is clearly attainable to each one of us. All it takes is determination to do what is right, the will to see it through, and a heart willing to receive God's strength and guidance. With God, *all* things are possible.

Emily Dickinson, in my opinion America's greatest poetess, wrote a great deal about this gap between what each of us is and what each of us *could* become. She concluded that if we fail to be heroic, we can blame no one but ourselves:

> We never know how high we are
> Till we are asked to rise
> And then if we are true to plan
> Our statures touch the skies—
>
> The Heroism we recite
> Would be a normal thing
> Did not ourselves the Cubits warp
> For fear to be a King!
> —"We Never Know How High,"
> Emily Dickinson, 1830–1886

About This Collection

It's hard to see how one could put together a collection of hero stories more powerful than these, for they are *la crème de la crème* of genre stories over a period of a century or more. Many are certifiably true, easy to so identify, and I'd guess that a number of the fictional ones were based on true prototype accounts.

Four of the stories are about famous people who lived noble lives of service to others and who searched for ways to make life more meaningful and beautiful: "God's Eager Fool" (Albert Schweitzer); "The Bird Man" (John James Audubon); "War on Yellow Fever" (Dr. Walter Reed); and "The Luminous World of Helen Keller." Three of these four willingly risked their very lives on behalf of others or for mankind.

Four other stories, "Coals of Fire," "One Suffering One," "Huldah Dean's Heroism," and "Girl Against a Blizzard" have children or teenagers as protagonists.

One story, "Hero in Feathers," reminds us that even animals can be heroic, willing to pay the ultimate price for those they love.

Another, "A Matter of Honor," tells of a young man whose sense of honor and integrity electrified a community of business leaders.

Six stories, "Aunt Becky's Boys, "He Knew Lincoln," "A New Celebration of Memorial Day," "The Way of the Cross, "Platte River Rhapsody," and "The Answer" have to do with quiet, unassuming people who nevertheless led heroic lives.

Five of the stories feature ordinary people who were willing to not only lay their reputations on the line, but even to give up their very lives in order that others might live: "Heroes of Today," "Coals of Fire," "Girl Against a Blizzard," "The Radio Notwithstanding," and "Crumpled Wings."

Some of the authors—such as Arthur Gordon and Arthur Milward—are still writing; others—such as Margaret E. Sangster Jr., John Scott Douglas, Van Wyck Brooks, Martha F. Simmonds, Mary Brownly, G. E. Wallace, and John A. O'Brien—were well-known scholars and writers earlier in this century.

Of the others, little is known today.

CODA

It is my hope that this collection of stories about men, women, and children whose lives are worth emulating will prove to be an inspiration and a source of courage wherever it is read. If you know of additional stories with the same emotive power as these, I would deeply appreciate your sending me copies with information about authorship, date, and place of earliest publication, if known. As I edit collections of stories in other genres, I welcome any story that fits our criteria. I would also appreciate hearing your response to the stories in this collection. You may reach me by writing to:

Joe L. Wheeler, Ph.D.
c/o WaterBrook Press
2375 Telstar Drive, Suite 160
Colorado Springs, CO 80920

ONE

HEROES OF TODAY

Ruth Lees Olson

Ben Tilden had twice done his classmate John Hanewald a terrible wrong—and John had paid a heavy price for those wrongs. And now, Ben's unprincipled acts had finally caught up with him. Only one thing could save that vindictive life; fortunately, John had been expressly forbidden to even consider that one thing.

I first read this story half a century ago, and it made such an impact on me that it has stayed in my conscious mind through the years. There was no question at all about it: It *had* to anchor this book.

A *laboratory* technician! Fine chance to develop heroism in this place! The young man laid aside the book he was reading and continued his soliloquy. *This writer says that "every individual has an opportunity, at least once in a lifetime, to be a hero." He may think this is true, but there are exceptions to every rule. Those of us who must travel the prosaic road of life know that it takes opportunities to develop heroes. And the winged fellow who is supposed to represent all this does not visit hospital laboratories. If it was a new kind of germ that needed to be caught and labeled, we might find it, but—a hero? Please call the surgical ward in the hospital!* So mused John Augustus Hanewald.

John Augustus was not a chemist from choice, but "the destiny that shapes our ends, rough hew them as we will," had drawn the lines of necessity so tightly that the young man was forced to take advantage of the first opening that came his way to make a livelihood. That was in the laboratory-pharmacy of a large hospital.

That usually quiet half-hour at the end of his day's work was conducive to retrospection, and John found himself thinking that he might have been a hero after all had not Ben Tilden's father persuaded his father to sign as security on a note for a large sum of money, then failed to meet the obligation when the note fell due, thus leaving Mr. Hanewald to pay the indebtedness. Doing so had forced him into bankruptcy, and in consequence he lost everything he owned.

The loss of his father's fortune brought a still greater hardship to the young man when it came time for him to enter college. He had set his heart on becoming a doctor, and that necessitated premedical work. Ben Tilden had no financial burdens to carry. His wealthy grandmother paid all his bills. But John was obliged to earn every cent of his expenses, and it was a hard, steady grind, with little to lighten the burden.

Only one star of hope shone brightly on the horizon of the future. That was the possibility of his winning the Stanhope Scholarship Prize. If he could accomplish this, it would mean his first year in medical school would be free from financial worries. True, a number of students had entered the race, including Ben Tilden, but John was working on the requirements with might and main, and he had faith in his ability to win. Many an hour when the

young man should have been asleep was spent on his thesis. His teachers congratulated him on his exceptionally fine daily work, and he had a good right to expect a reward. But "the best laid schemes o' mice and men gang aft a-gley." The afternoon when the final papers were to be handed in, John's thesis mysteriously disappeared. He had left it in the desk in his room, and the desk was locked! There was no indication that the lock had been tampered with, and no one seemed to know anything about it.

The dean made searching inquiries when the loss was reported, but to no avail. There was no time for John to rewrite the thesis, and when the great moment came, he found himself sitting in the audience listening to a ceremony which awarded the prize he had prayed for and wished for and worked for and deserved, to Ben Tilden, who did not need it and who had wanted it only because of the $5,000 check his grandmother had promised him in addition to his expenses if he won. So by hook or crook Ben simply *had* to win. But John felt sure that his competitor had won by crook, and that he could throw light on the whereabouts of the missing thesis if he so wished.

Premedic graduation came and went. Ben Tilden entered upon his medical course and John Augustus Hanewald took a special course in chemistry, a subject in which he had been much interested all through his school days. His heart was still set on being a doctor, but he knew that it would be some years at least before he could hope to collect the necessary cash, and in the meantime, this work would be good experience.

In fact, three years had passed since John had entered the Princeton Hospital laboratory. He had made many friends in the medical fraternity, and really enjoyed his work, for it was to him only a stepping stone to higher things. Some day—he was *sure* of this—he would reach his goal. As the thought of his ambition realized flashed across his mind, Hanewald smiled. He could forget and forgive Ben Tilden in that contemplation. Then glancing down at his folded hands, his brows drew together in a heavy frown. He could forgive, but would he?

Ben Tilden was graduated in medicine, and by irony of fate, entered Princeton Hospital for his intern work. He made himself rather officious when he could, and discovering John Hanewald, came frequently to the window of the laboratory and made suggestions as to how things should be managed, and how the stock should be arranged.

As completely as possible, John ignored him, and once even hinted that there was plenty of work for doctors in the wards. After that, Ben made himself even more obnoxious. One day, when John returned from lunch, he found this fledgling doctor in the laboratory. How he had gained entrance was a mystery, for the door was locked. But finding John absent, and the moment apparently opportune to try out a pet theory of his own, he gained an entrance—somehow—and now had several shelves misarranged. He was in the act of setting down a large bottle of acid when John opened the door and entered. Evidently the intruder did not expect the chemist to return so soon, for in confusion he mumbled something about needing a formula filled, and finding no one there, he decided to make it up himself.

There was a sharp note of anger in John's voice as he answered, "You have no business in here, Ben Tilden. You know very well it is against the rules of the hospital, and it will go hard with you if I report your meddling with chemical supplies."

There was a sneer on Tilden's face as he whirled to confront John. But the words that trembled on his tongue were never uttered, for his elbow struck the bottle he had just taken from the shelf, upsetting it. John reached out to catch it, but too late to save a catastrophe. The neck struck a mortar standing near, and the burning acid splashed out over his hand and arm. But only a few sprinkles fell on Ben's clothes.

It was the sight of the ugly scars just healing and the memory of the pain so recently borne that brought the frown to the young man's face as he sat there in the laboratory in the gloaming. The sound of a distant clock brought him back to realities, and with a sigh he arose and put away the book, *Heroes of Today*.

He walked over to the window and stood gazing at the feathery snowflakes dancing through the air in mad glee, touching lightly the cheeks of the passers-by or spreading their snowy skirts to cover the ugly brown of sidewalk and street. There was the usual busy throng of people and cars on the avenue several stories below his window. *This surely is a night for careful driving,* he murmured to himself as the automobiles dashed around the corners and raced across intersections. *Oh, well,* he shrugged, *I have no worries about that kind of transportation. A good walk is a fine blood purifier, and I know it will give me an appetite for whatever is set before me. Mother won't complain about my eating tonight.*

John Augustus was late in rising the next morning, so had only a few moments left to scan the paper. What he saw when he opened it brought an exclamation to his lips. "TERRIBLE ACCIDENT," the bold headlines read. "Prominent young doctor badly injured." Yes, it was Ben Tilden. He had tried to beat the other automobile across the intersection. Both cars were wrecked, and the other driver hurt slightly. But Ben was in the hospital with but a faint chance for life.

John thought of several things as he pulled his glove over his scarred hand and started for work. If Ben Tilden had played the game square, this thing might not have happened. But now what would be the outcome? A little prayer of thanksgiving to God for His love and protecting care, and a sincere wish that Ben might live, even if his ways were to be despised by a straightforward, upstanding fellow, flitted through John's thoughts and left him in a more charitable mood as he reached the hospital.

In the early afternoon, one of the leading physicians of the city came to the laboratory. John was very well acquainted with Dr. Wallace, for he had done considerable work for him, and more than once they had both enjoyed heart-to-heart talks about the young chemist's cherished desires and ambitions. "What is it now, Doctor?" he asked.

There was a look of anxiety in the eyes that gazed into his own. "A blood transfusion, Hanewald. I wish you would give the work your careful attention. Success means the saving of a life."

"Who is it?" questioned John, more as a matter of form than from a real interest. The answer, however, went through him like an electric shock.

"I thought you knew," answered the doctor in some surprise. "Young Tilden, who is interning here. He was in an automobile accident last night, and has lost altogether too much blood."

"I'll do my best," John's voice sounded strange even to his own ears.

The doctor went out to complete his rounds, and John stood with a dazed look on his face for several moments. Ben Tilden was his enemy! But after all, he did not want to see him die. Oh, no! Could he find someone whose blood matched that of the young intern? That was his problem now.

John had given of his own blood twice that year to save others. He might have answered a similar call for help the previous week, save that he had been forbidden to do so by the chief of the hospital staff. "It might bring serious results, Hanewald," the busy doctor had explained, "and we cannot risk losing you. You are too valuable a man. Do not consider any more transfusions for at least three months, please."

Late that afternoon Dr. Wallace returned to the laboratory, and John knew at once that things were not going well. "How is Tilden?" he asked.

"Low, very low," came the quick response. "Unless we can give him a transfusion tonight he will slip through our fingers. His grandmother has offered a nice sum of money to anyone who will give the blood. But, of course, it must match Tilden's. That's the catch. I received your report. What can we do, Hanewald? Have you any suggestions?"

John felt as though an icy hand had gripped his heart. He busied himself with some test tubes for a few minutes, then he answered, "Come back in half an hour, Doctor. It may be I can find someone for you by that time."

Dr. Wallace looked keenly at the figure bent over the table, but there was nothing in the young man's expression that revealed the thoughts that filled his mind. "All right. And I hope you succeed. It's the only possible chance for saving a life." As he left the room, John found himself repeating the words again and again, "Saving a life. Saving a life."

Reluctantly he made a test of his own blood, almost praying that it might be negative. And he reasoned, as he worked, *My life is my own, and no one has a right to ask anything of me that will impair its usefulness in any way. I'm not responsible for any man's carelessness, and why should I be concerned or take any risk? It's neither fair nor just. And yet,* Dr. Wallace's words rang in his ears: *Saving a life…*

As he looked at the result of his test, he knew what he must do, but still he stood for several minutes rapt in thought, trying to make a final decision.

At last he called his assistant to take charge of the laboratory, and picking up his hat, left the building. A walk in the fresh air would give him courage and strength. He walked several blocks to a little park and sat down on a bench. The fight with himself was not quite over yet. Suddenly he became aware that children were talking near him. He could not see them, for they were on the other side of a column of evergreens, but he could hear the conversation very plainly.

"I tell you, Nito, you cannot be bad to Frankie no more."

"Yis I can," replied a boyish voice. "Frankie, he one bad boy. He break my wagon and I goin' ter feex him."

"No!" and the word was spoken with emphasis. "I, your sister, tell you that the lady angel of our mission say, 'You must forgive your enemies, and be good to them what break up your wagon!'" Evidently the boy was not convinced, for he said, "Who cares what your lady angel says? I goin' ter beat up on Frankie."

The girl began her argument from another angle. "You cannot come to our mission if you fight, for Jesus tells you to love everybody. Jesus never fights."

The boy was undecided. "What your lady angel give me to be good?" he queried shrewdly.

Before the girl could answer, a park policeman appeared on the scene, and the boy ran across the drifted snow and down a side street.

John Hanewald determined to make the acquaintance of the child who had stood so courageously for the right; so he passed around the evergreens and came face to face with a crippled girl in an old apology for a wheelchair.

He raised his hat with courtly grace as he asked, "What became of your brother?"

She shook her head. "I guess he run away. He scared of policeman. But they is always good to me. Do you think Nito will ever learn to love my Jesus?"

"Yes, I think he will, especially if his little sister keeps her faith in Him," the stranger answered with a smile. "But tell me about yourself." During the conversation which followed, she grew confidential.

"Nito, my brother, is older, so he carry me around when I be little. But one day he run fast with the boys, and he drop me hard, so I don't ever walk again. But," she added hastily, "Nito, he not mean to me, and I love my brother oh, so much."

"Poor child! But he crippled you for life, and now you cannot run and jump like other girls."

"He very sorry, but I never let him say one word about it. When you love people, you don't be bad to them."

"No, I guess you don't," mused John. "But if you have no love in your heart for them—well, that's different."

Bidding his new friend adieu, John Augustus Hanewald returned to Princeton Hospital. As he mounted the steps, he thought, *That crippled girl had real hero stuff in her. Surely if a child from the slums, doomed to be a cripple for life, can forgive and forget, why not a strong man who has suffered less than half of that?*

Dr. Wallace came hurrying down the corridor as the young man stopped at his office door. He inquired anxiously, "Did you find anyone, Hanewald? We haven't a moment to lose."

"Yes," came the quiet answer, "and everything is ready."

Together they went over to the laboratory. But when the doctor found out who was to give the blood transfusion, he objected strenuously. "I cannot let you make this sacrifice, John, for that is what it is. I happen to know that you have been forbidden to give any more blood for three months. Remember, your own life is at stake. The world, with all its needs, waits for your service. If Tilden recovers, he will be at best only a wreck of a man. No, Hanewald, you cannot give *your* blood to him. I will not accept it."

John laid his hand gently on the surgeon's arm. "Listen, Dr. Wallace. Your patient, Ben Tilden, once—yes, twice—did me a great wrong—never mind what—but ever since I have hated him, and vowed that some day I would get even. In the last hour I have learned the real meaning of a Bible verse I had forgotten. There is no longer any rancor in my heart. I am willing to pay the price, for 'greater love hath no man than this, that a man lay down his life for his friend.'"

The next day John lay in a hospital bed, his face as white as his pillows. There was a quiet peacefulness in his heart. He was "even" with Ben at last. The door opened softly, and Dr. Wallace entered.

"So they obeyed my orders and put you to bed. Well, here you stay for a week. Not a word—" the physician laid his hand over the young man's lips. "I'm doing the talking now. I came in to say two things. First, the transfusion was a success, and the patient will recover. Second, Ben Tilden's grandmother sent you this," and he held up a slip of blue paper. "I'm making the deposit for you in the bank myself, and adding enough to your credit to see you through medical school. We need such young men as you in the medical profession."

"But, Doctor—" the patient struggled to speak.

"Not a word! Not a word! My boy, you are a real hero!" And the man of medicine was gone.

With a smile on his lips and a high resolve in his heart, John Augustus Hanewald fell asleep to dreams of joys to come.

RUTH LEES OLSON *wrote for inspirational and family magazines during the first half of the twentieth century.*

Two

ONE SUFFERING ONE

Arthur A. Milward

Billy would never walk again, let alone run, jump, play soccer, or do any of the other things that made his life worth living—at least he couldn't...until he met Valerie.

Arthur A. Milward, a professional writer who has been published many times in *Reader's Digest,* remembers a tremendous lesson in courage in that children's hospital in London.

She didn't have red hair or freckles, but somehow she reminded me of a combination of Peppermint Patty and a little red-haired girl. She had the contrasting qualities of courage and innocent appeal.

She was about ten or twelve years old. It was hard to be sure of her age from her appearance, as her stunted, malformed frame made her look younger than she was. But her small oval face wore an expression more appropriate to a grown woman.

Her eyes were her dominant feature. Large, dark, and luminous, fringed by long, thick lashes, they were her one beauty. She had the habit of gazing steadily for a long moment at a newcomer to the children's ward. If she liked what she saw, her face would light up and she would shuffle over and introduce herself.

She had a smile, the nurses said, that could light up a room—and could make you forget her misshapen body and painful, awkward movements.

She smiled often. I never saw her cry, although she had experienced a great deal of pain, rejection, and disappointment. Valerie, I gathered, had already shed all her tears several years and countless operations ago.

Valerie would come to the children's surgical ward for prolonged periods. Then she would disappear, only to return within a few months for further corrective surgery—surgery that could only, at best, make life manageable for her. She had MBD—multiple birth defects.

Valerie had a well-developed and slightly cynical sense of humor. When some unthinking visitor would ask what was wrong with her, she would smile sweetly and suggest that he return later when he had a day off work and time to spare. "But," she would add innocently, "if you're in a hurry, I can tell you what's right with me."

Whenever she was recovering from one of her operations, Valerie would "fall" out of her bed—which was the only way she could manage to get out of bed without help (and she scorned help). She would shuffle around the ward, helping to care for the other children.

The small patients liked Valerie in spite of her appearance and curious method of maneuvering. She could get them to do things even when the nurses failed.

Valerie stood for no nonsense. Pain was a fact of life as far as she was concerned. And she had, in her small, misshapen frame, enough courage for a wardful of children.

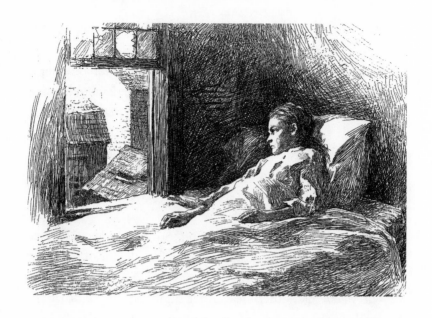

Valerie's parents didn't visit her every day, as many of the other children's parents did. Possibly her parents were both working or had other children to care for. They came once or twice a week, and Valerie didn't seem to care very much whether her mother came or not. A young, fashionably dressed woman, her mother always seemed to be in a hurry. She invariably gave an impression of embarrassment, and she sort of disassociated herself from her daughter when other parents stopped by.

But Valerie's father, on the other hand, was outgoing and affectionate. He would wait at the end of the ward for Valerie to shuffle across to meet him, her face lit up. He always greeted her in the same way. "Hi there, beautiful," he'd call. He made it sound as if he really meant it. And just for a moment, as the little girl reached the end of her shuffling run toward him, dropped her canes, and fell into his arms, he was right.

Then one cold and windy autumn night Billy came into the ward. Actually, it was very early in the morning, before dawn. He came up from emergency surgery, the victim of a car wreck on the M-2 Expressway.

His parents were relatively unhurt, but Billy had been pinned in the wreckage for a long time. He had severe injuries to his lower legs. The doctor's prognosis was that eight-year-old Billy had taken his last steps.

Billy was sunk in deep depression. So now he would never walk again, let alone run, jump, play soccer, or do any of the other things that made his life worth living.

But Valerie had other ideas. After summing up the situation, she decided that the prognosis was nonsense. "The kid'll walk," she declared. She'd been there. She knew.

When, fairly well along in his convalescence, Billy still refused to get out of bed, put his feet on the floor, and try to stand, Valerie took over his case. After breakfast one morning she issued her first directive: "Out of that bed, kid; it's time to get up!"

Billy tearfully protested that he couldn't walk. He demanded that she go away and leave him alone. But by sheer force of will she coaxed him out of his bed and into an upright position, then into the metal walker.

She spent exhausting hours with him every day. And at the end of the day she would crumple into an untidy heap on the floor. She'd be asleep before a nurse came by to lift her onto her bed.

She put up with all kinds of abuse from her unwilling patient. Once, early in the rehabilitation program, Billy lost his temper and stormed at her, "Valerie, why can't you leave me alone? What do *you* know? You're weird."

Valerie stopped dead. Her oval face went white and her chin quivered. She looked as close to tears as I ever saw her. But only for a moment. Then she stuck out her chin and fixed the boy with her eyes.

"I know it," she said. "But I can't help it—and you *can!* Come on." After that, things went better. Billy became more cooperative.

Some weeks later he began to share her faith that he would recover. He became enthusiastic, and the two children grew to be best friends.

Then, close to three months after he'd entered the hospital, Billy closed the curtains around his bed. He dressed himself in the new suit his excited parents had brought, packed his things into his small suitcase, and walked with his family to the parking lot in front of the hospital.

———————

Valerie and some staff workers were there. Billy, grinning from ear to ear, turned and waved. Everyone waved back except Valerie. She couldn't. She needed both hands on her canes to support herself. Her face showed no sign of emotion, but her tiny knuckles clutching the handles of her walking canes were very white. The contrast was hard to bear. The excited, happy little boy who had learned to walk again, and the tiny, misshapen girl who would never walk properly.

Billy got into the car with his parents and young sister. And with a final wave he was gone.

Onlookers and hospital staff stood staring out into the courtyard, unwilling to move.

"Valerie was the first to speak. "Well," she said, "what are we all staring at? There's work to be done. Come on, it's time to get trays round for supper."

———

In heaven Valerie will walk straight and tall. She will walk without tiring, and she won't fall down.

ARTHUR A. MILWARD *was born in England and later immigrated to America. Besides his career in printing, he has a second career—writing. A number of his true stories have been carried all over the world by* Reader's Digest. *Today, Mr. Milward lives and writes from Kennett Square, Pennsylvania.*

THREE

GOD'S EAGER FOOL

John A. O'Brien

He was a legend in his own time—a world-renowned Bible scholar, a great concert organist, and an author of a definitive biography of J. S. Bach. Why then would he give all of this up and go back to school again, just to throw his life away in one of the most disease-plagued spots on this planet?

When asked why he'd be such a fool, Dr. Albert Schweitzer reached back almost two thousand years for his answer.

———

To be a fool for God, a man must forsake the comforts of the world and spend his life in service to others. For nearly forty years Albert Schweitzer has been just that kind of fool.

It began in the market square at Colmar, in Upper Alsace. Schweitzer stood frowning up at the statue of a naked Negro. The submissive black figure, carved on a monument erected to Admiral Bruat and to French colonial power, seemed to Schweitzer to symbolize man's inhumanity to man.

Can it be true, as I have heard, he mused, *'that we exploit these black people and do not give them even doctors or medicine?*

On the way home to Strasbourg the dark image gave him no peace.

But why should my conscience be troubled? he argued. *I am a university professor, not a missionary.* He might have added that, at thirty, he had achieved fame in three fields: he was a world-renowned biblical scholar; as a concert organist, he was a favorite of Continental and British audiences; and he had written an outstanding biography of Bach.

Then he happened to read a magazine article about the Congo: "While we are preaching to these natives about religion, they are suffering and dying from physical maladies, for which we missionaries can do nothing."

What Schweitzer felt then he later wrote: "A heavy guilt rests upon us for what the whites of all nations have done to the colored peoples. When we do good to them, it is not benevolence—it is atonement."

And the scholar-musician made a vow to spend the rest of his life atoning to jungle savages. His friends protested: If the aborigines of Africa needed help, let Schweitzer raise money for their assistance. He certainly was not called upon to wash lepers with his own hands!

Schweitzer answered by quoting Goethe: "In the beginning was the Deed!"

His beginning deed was to enter medical school. Nearly five years later, when he was about to be graduated as physician and surgeon, he found himself involved in what might have been a staggering complication. The man of heroic purpose had fallen in love! His friends exulted: Marriage, they felt sure, would end his impractical scheme.

But Helene Bresslau, daughter of a Jewish historian at the University of Strasbourg, had known his plans from the beginning. To

her he had bluntly proposed: "I am studying to be a doctor for savages. Would you spend all the rest of your life with me—in the jungle?"

And she had answered: "I shall become a trained nurse. Then how could you go without me?"

They both knew that in tropical forests a medical diploma would not be enough; one must have medicines, bandages, surgical instruments. So Schweitzer lectured and wrote and played himself thin to earn money for the expedition.

On Good Friday of 1913, he and his bride left for Cape Lopez, in French Equatorial Africa. There the travelers found their first African friend, Joseph, who had once worked as cook for a white family. In canoes, Joseph guided the doctor and his wife on a three-day journey up the Ogowe River to the mission post at Lambaréné. This was the heart of the disease-cursed territory of which he had read, where the death rate was mounting every year. It was a world swarming with billions of tsetse flies, ants, termites, and disease-laden mosquitoes.

When at last they reached Lambaréné, Dr. Schweitzer looked at his wife in dismay. They had been promised sleeping quarters and a two-room hospital of corrugated iron—not even a shack was ready for them! Where to store delicate surgical tools that rust so quickly in the tropics? Where to unpack life-giving medicines?

Quickly they pitched camp, covered instruments with grease, and, to keep medicines from spoiling, buried the bottles in the earth near deep, cool springs. Of these queer activities the natives were instantly suspicious. Naked men who looked like the statue in Colmar gathered around campfires, while out of the deeper forest came the Pygmies, and then the Fangs and the Zendehs, whose teeth are filed to sharp points for eating human flesh.

Joseph insisted the confab was ominous; tribal magicians were preaching hatred and distrust of the newcomers. But Schweitzer, watching from a distance, saw that many of the natives were crawling with disease: swamp fever and sleeping sickness and a hundred tropical ailments.

"Let's get to work!" the doctor called. "Bring sick people here."

In desperation Schweitzer took over an abandoned hen house—his first hospital. An old camp bed would be the operating table. Dirt on bed and walls was covered with whitewash.

The savages clustered round, their skin painted and tattooed in bright colors. The men toted spears and broad-bladed knives, and some clutched crossbows of ebony, the arrows tipped with venom. Before this menacing audience, Schweitzer confronted his first patients, hardy souls who volunteered to try the white man's magic.

A man with a chronic pain in his right side agrees to lie on the cot. They curtain in the surgery, but through big holes in the roof, as the operation for appendicitis is begun, gleaming eyes peer from a leafy amphitheater...

Suppose the patient dies? What will these tribesmen do then?

Now it is over. Thank God, the patient groans and opens his eyes. From the jungle point of view, the operation is an instantaneous triumph; did they not behold this white wizard kill a native, cut open his innards and then bring the corpse back to life? Now the natives willingly help to build the hospital; swiftly on the edge of the hill, above the threat of the flooding river, rise three rooms—examination, ward, and surgery.

As word of the white magician spread through the jungle, natives trudged from afar, eager to be killed and brought back to life. Schweitzer operated for boils, hernias, tumors and for large tropical ulcers that grow on naked feet. To care for such ulcers took weeks, sometimes months; meanwhile the patients camped at the hospital door, and feeding them was a problem. Some grateful relatives brought in fowl, eggs, or bananas, but others even expected presents for themselves. Often the natives, if they liked the taste of a medicine, would steal the bottle and at one sitting drink the whole supply.

To be sure of food, Schweitzer cleared a space in the jungle and planted a truck garden and a plantation for fruit and palm oil trees. Beads and calico he traded for bananas and tapioca. But to live off the land alone was impossible; rice, meat, butter, and potatoes must be expensively imported from Europe.

In spite of the many difficulties, the good physician began to win the hearts of the tribesmen. In the first year, not one patient died, and thousands were relieved of pain. Like an apostle to the deeper jungle, Schweitzer made journeys of mercy on foot to distant Negro tribes.

That he did not crumple under the strain of these prodigious labors was due, Schweitzer explains, to a jungle paradox—a zinc-lined, tropic-proof piano, gift of the Paris Bach Society. At night when the physician's work was done, the musician, the expert on Bach, would go to the keyboard and, against the diapason of wild forest sounds, let his fingers wander through stern and noble music. One night, lost in a transport of harmony, he feels a hand on his shoulder. His wife is pointing at the open window. Shadows are creeping toward the door of the sick ward. The doctor groans. Zendehs, confound them! Cannibals, hoping to kidnap a helpless sick man and carry him off for tomorrow's dinner!

Seizing a shotgun, the doctor fires a noisy blast at the sky. The terrified man-eaters scatter and flee...

In August 1914, French officers appeared at the doctor's door and took him prisoner.

"War has come to Europe," they said. "You are Germans."

"No, we are Alsatians. We are working here to offset German oppression—"

But official stupidity had its way; the Schweitzers were shipped back to Europe and confined in an internment camp. When the war was ended, they were very ill; doctors warned them never to go back to Africa.

After three years of recuperation Schweitzer felt well enough to barnstorm Europe and the British Isles, giving organ concerts and lectures to raise money for his jungle mission. He traveled third class, lived in cheap hotels, and saved every sou. By 1924 he had capital enough to resume his work. Helene was still too ill to travel with him, but she would follow when she could.

In the years between, heat and white ants had eaten up all that Schweitzer had built in Lambaréné. He must begin all over again. In the mornings he must be a doctor; in the afternoons, a builder. And he must try to forget the loneliness and the blinding, sickening heat. But again grateful natives pitched in to help the rebuilding, and a Catholic mission farther up the river sent to the Protestant doctor a skilled carpenter.

Soon Schweitzer could write to his supporters in Europe that deaths in the great forest were going down. A little later he could tell them that leprosy had been wonderfully checked; only about fifty thousand cases remained, one in sixty! "Send us medicine, send us food, for the love of God!" was his constant plea.

At last, after long years, Helene rejoined her husband. The prospects looked bright for the mission. They had a three-hundred-bed hospital, with a dispensary, a modern operating room and a laboratory, a lying-in ward and nursery.

The very latest improvements were electrification (with the doctor doing the wiring) and new wards for the insane. By order of the witch doctors, hapless lunatics are drowned in the river. At Lambaréné, Schweitzer began to practice elementary psychiatry, and some of his dark paranoiacs even got well.

Then war exploded again in Europe, posing a bitter problem. Dr. Schweitzer faced his wife, and, as always, Helen's answer was ready:

"We must not try to escape. The poor sick blacks depend upon us. It is a matter of conscience."

This time they were not disturbed.

How did they survive the war years, cut off as they were from regular supply sources? That, too, is a miracle story. Friends in the United States went to work—the Unitarian Service Committee, the General Council of Congregational Churches, helpers in the Protestant Episcopal Church, American organists, and many others collected cash and food and medicines, turning it all over to Professor Everett Skillings of Middlebury College in Vermont, treasurer of the Albert Schweitzer Fellowship. Dr. Edward H. Hume of the Christian Medical Council for Overseas Work found ships to transport the precious cargoes.

Letters that came from Lambaréné told of the almost inexpressible fatigue of husband and wife. To withstand that tropical inferno, a European needs to go home once every two years; yet since 1939 Schweitzer had not left the hospital. Writing late in 1945, he spoke of how impossible it was to leave the mission; so much to be done. (The Schweitzers did at last leave and visit the United States briefly in the summer of 1949.)

During those trying years Dr. Schweitzer found time to write two large volumes on philosophy.

What *is* the philosophy of such a man? For all his scholarly profundity, he believes in simple things.

"There is," he writes, "an essential sanctity of the human personality, regardless of race or color or conditions of life. If that ideal is abandoned, the intellectual man goes to pieces and that means the end of culture and even of humanity."

Another conviction—indeed, the guiding principle of Schweitzer's life—is the supremacy of Christ's commandment to love. "Only through love," he says, "can we attain to communion with God!"

Nearly two thousand years ago Saint Paul spoke of those who are "fools for Christ's sake." Since then many men and women have marched down history, yielding up the comforts of life to serve their fellow men. With that bright company today goes that eager fool for God—Albert Schweitzer.

JOHN A. O'BRIEN *wrote for popular magazines during the mid-twentieth century.*

FOUR

AUNT BECKY'S BOYS

Carrie B. Ilsey

Heroes come in many sizes and shapes—none more unlikely or more glorious than the old woman in the tattered old coat that vainly tried to protect her from the winter's cold.

Aunt Becky, who refused to rest until every last one of her boys had taken that one crucial step.

Aunt Becky's little brown house, like her tanned and wrinkled face, had withstood the winter's winds and summer's drought on the unchanging prairie ever since anybody could remember. In her flower garden she planted the zinnias, marigolds, and four-o'clocks in the same beds where her mother had planted them, and rested under the shade of the trees her father had set out all such a long, long time ago. For this was Aunt Becky's childhood home, the only home she had ever known. Here she had become a bride and a mother, and here too one by one she laid all she loved best to sleep under the hill just beyond her window, where every morning she watched the first warm rays of the sun kiss the cold slabs above her head.

The old house was empty now, except for her, but she had long since grown used to the silence. Sometimes, to be sure, she was lonely—oh, so lonely! And yes, sometimes she wept, though not when any eye could see, for just as her neighbors set their clocks by the light in her window every morning, so they set their lives by the sunlight in her dear old face.

Rheumatic pains often stiffened Aunt Becky's joints, and at such times she wondered if her race were about run. Not that she minded going out on the hillside yonder for her last long sleep, but she really wanted to stay in the world till she felt her work was really finished. She wasn't one to lay down her tools until she had accomplished the purpose for which she had taken them in hand, and she had one unfinished task, dear to her heart through many a long year.

Long, long ago, when the deep furrows that now seamed her face were laughing dimples, and brown curls clustered instead of sparse silver waves, Aunt Becky had volunteered, because nobody else would, to take a class of boisterous boys—young savages, they were considered by some—as her share of the Sunday school work. Her heart failed her once and she decided to give them up, but her friends reminded her, "You wanted them, Becky; now you keep them"—and keep them she did, twelve of them. They became known as Aunt Becky's boys, and would have rioted forthwith had any one dared to dispute the honor. Aunt Becky didn't scold; Aunt Becky didn't mind muddy feet and uncouth ways, and by some magic all her own she never failed to know whether it was a boy's soul or his stomach that was hungry.

This turbulent little pool of humanity had emptied itself, little by little, into the big ocean of life, but Aunt Becky never forgot her boys, and many a comforting message from them solaced her lonely hours. They were not all Christians when they left her, but she counted her earthly mission incomplete until she was absolutely certain that each had entered that promised land where all giants of wrongdoing had been conquered and the soul fed on the grapes of righteousness.

It was revival time in the old meeting house, and a bright moon lighted all the highways and byways to the town. The church, to be sure, had acquired a new front and a tower and other improvements, but the heart of it was still the old church, which Aunt Becky's own hands had helped to erect. How she loved it! Every inch of the solid timbers which her brethren of pioneer days had felled and hauled over new-broken roads, heartened to the task by the labors of the women. They were all gone now, all but Aunt Becky, and she felt a peculiar ownership in this temple of the Lord, scarcely possible for any of the others. She felt, as the years had taught her to feel, that no service of worship was complete without her presence.

When the revival crowds filled the sanctuary, Aunt Becky was always one of the number. She was all eyes and ears one night when the evangelist said, at the close of his sermon, "What man is there here who has courage enough to step out first, acknowledging that he's been a wanderer from the Lord and wants to come home?" Down the gallery steps, down the aisle, pushing his way through the crowd in his eagerness to enter the sanctuary, came a tall well-dressed stranger whom nobody seemed to know.

"Our friend's name is Gordon," the evangelist began to explain, when a queer little noise on Aunt Becky's side of the room attracted a bit of attention her way, though few could understand the rapture in the wrinkled old face. Its owner had an individuality all her own, and was used to doing things as her inner self prompted. The evangelist didn't even have time to complete his sentence before the little woman stood in front of the stranger, grasping both his hands in hers, and looking up at the tall form with an exultation that defied description. Then in a voice broken with glad emotion she cried: "O Tip, I just knew you'd come some day! I knew it! I knew it! For I've asked the Lord for you so many times!" A sudden sound of emotion rippling through the audience prevented Tip's greeting from being heard, but no eye failed to see him lean down to kiss her cheek.

"Must be one of Aunt Becky's Sabbath school boys come back," was the explanation offered by some of the older people in the congregation.

"Tell me, Tip; be honest with me, boy, as you used to do," Aunt Becky implored later when the meeting was over. "What was it that made you run off and stay all these years, and why didn't you write to the folks? Why, many a time your poor mother has mourned you for dead."

"Ah, I know it, Aunt Becky, only too well." A flush spread across the handsome face. "But it was this way: I was young and full of mischief, and somehow I felt that you and mother were giving me too big a dose of religion, all put together, and I decided to leave it all behind me. But, do you know, I never could forget, hard as I tried?"

"Why, of course, we knew that all the time, you rascal."

"The other night, in our home five hundred miles from here, a little lad whom my wife and I have taken to raise, climbed on my knee and asked, 'Poor daddy, are you just like me? Don't you have any really-truly papa or mama?" That settled the matter. I just *had* to come and set things right with you and Mother and—and—the Lord."

The kerosene light burned late that evening in the brown cottage while its sole occupant searched every one of her treasure hiding places. At last she found the object of her quest—a much-bethumbed record book bearing a date forty years gone by. Aunt Becky knew as well before she opened it as she did afterward what was in it, but the experience of the evening stirred old memories down in lost forgotten recesses of her faithful heart, and she felt she must look at the old roll once more to make sure that time had not played any tricks with her mental powers. The twelve boys whose names were recorded on the first page were not the only ones, by a long shot, whom she had taught and sought to influence, but these lads made up her original class, and whatever she might or might not do for others, her vow, made when she took them, ever confronted her: She must present these twelve as an unbroken band as her offering to her Master.

The firelight flickered over the worn furnishings of the high-ceilinged room, and faces of other generations looked down from the walls, on this remnant of their race who seemed to defy time and sat with all the alertness and intentness of youth scrutinizing her record.

"Toby Bates," she read. "God bless little Toby." He was a sailor boy now, and he often wrote to Aunt Becky that he kept his Christian colors flying.

The old lady laughed outright at the remembrance of Tommy Bond's appetite, which never seemed to have enough to satisfy it except when it came to her table. She was proud of Tommy's record as a graduate engineer who never forgot his Lord. Proud, too, of Lee and Sam, God-fearing mechanics.

"The Deacon," whom the boys ridiculed, came next, and she dropped a tear on a postcard picture of a grave whose marble shaft read, *Ray Duncan, Friend of the Black Man.* Her tears changed to smiles at the succeeding line: "Billy Hines." A woman of Samaria was the mother of this homely, neglected child, whose starved soul thrilled to music. "I know he's whistling church tunes," Aunt Becky had declared when she learned that this humble day laborer was cheering thousands of soldiers in the World War, for someone had discovered he was a marvelous whistler.

Bud…Joe…Frizzy, she read on down the list, and wondered at the power which could transform such scamps into worthwhile men. Bud was now a physician who lived for others; Joe a lawyer who practiced the Golden Rule; and Frizzy a chief among the Gideons.

Bob Jacobs brought back tender reminiscences, but she didn't know his whereabouts. *Wish I knew if that rattle-brained Julius Smith ever amounted to anything,* she mused. Reuben White and John Thompson were in the old town, and were blessed with prosperity, but that didn't satisfy Aunt Becky, for they didn't know the Lord. The record dropped from her lap and the old lady slipped down to her knees.

There was no human ear to hear, and the worshiper let her voice rise full and clear and sweet in thanksgiving to her Lord. Then it broke and trailed off like the mournful soughing of the wind as she remembered her unworthiness. "Dear Lord," she was saying, "Thou knewest how little of this world's goods I have had to give back to Thee. All that I have had has been my poor self; these hands and these feet. But Thou knowest, Father, that of what I have had I have given unstintedly. And now, if it please Thee, before Thou dost lay me to rest, and surely the time cannot be long, grant me this one more request, that I may see, some way, some how, the last of my boys safe in Thy kingdom of love. I ask this now for Reuben, Julius, and John. Amen."

The following morning as Aunt Becky repaired her old winter coat she remarked to a neighbor who had come in that if she thought she could do any better service for the Lord if she had a new, stylish garment, she'd be tempted to pray for it. But she laughed the matter off with her accustomed jollity, not wishing anyone to know how much she was embarrassed by her shabby clothes, and went to answer a rap at the door. "My father told me to hunt up Aunt Becky," said a young man by way of introduction, "and I understand that I'm at the right place."

"Harold Jacobs you say you are? Bob's boy? Why, lad, I've held you on my knee many a time. Come in!" The door swung wide open.

What a forenoon that was! They had lunch together, followed by a walk to the cemetery on the hillside where the young man's mother lay. "Didn't ever know much about her." Tears glistened in Aunt Becky's eyes as she looked into those of the boy. "Sit down, lad, and let me tell you," she urged, and they rested beside the mound. "Your father being one of my boys," the narrator began, "of course I was interested in the romping, vivacious girl whom he loved. Before they were married I was at her home one day, and she was making a dress so she could go to a party that night. It was white flannel with the fuzzy side out—quite a dress for those days. Well, of course, I had to say what was on my mind, and I just looked at her real sweet and said, 'Daisy Summers, I hope you won't go to that wild dance tonight.' My, but she was mad all over in a minute, and gave me to understand in a very polite way that she could take care of her own business. Of course I didn't take offense at it, but I went home and right on my heels came Daisy, crying and asking me to forgive her rudeness. And, do you know, boy, she didn't go to the party that night! Pretty soon she was con- verted and baptized in the old creek over there," indicating the shallow stream that wound its sluggish way over the prairie. "And what's more, she used that same dress for a baptismal robe.

"What a beautiful Christian she made too! And you never heard about her death?" Aunt Becky's voice grew tender and sweet as she recalled old scenes. Harold was a little child of two when his mother died. He could scarcely remember his newborn sister and an unchristian father, with the mother love pleading for the husband to meet her and her babies in the glad morning when the King comes to claim His own.

"He's going to keep his promise, Aunt Becky." Something more than wholesome pride stirred in the young man's heart as he watched the little old lady drink in his words. "Dad's the best Sunday school superintendent in El Paso. And I'm one too, down at the mission; and Sis helps me."

At the service that evening a stranger was on the platform with greetings from his church to the evangelist. Aunt Becky didn't catch his name, and thought little of him until, when the invitation was given at the close, she saw him go to the rear of the church where, to her amazement, sat the Reuben and John for whom she had prayed the night previous. *Here I've been asking the Lord for those boys, and am surprised that He sent them to the church,* she rebuked herself inwardly. When the three men came to the altar together, those who knew Aunt Becky best realized something of her joy as they watched her radiant face. She was one of the first to take Reuben by the hand, while John drew her over to him to say, confidentially, "I told Reub the other day that I believed he and I were the only ones of all your old boys who were still numbered among the goats, and I thought it about time we got over to the right side of the fence. So when Julius here came and asked us, we couldn't refuse."

"Julius?" Aunt Becky looked up at the stranger.

"You don't know me, do you?" he asked.

"Julius Smith, is it really you? And a church deacon at that? Well, this is the first time I've ever known that any word of mine ever lodged in your rattly brain."

"O Aunt Becky, it wasn't your words, but it was your patience and your smile that I always thought of when I was tempted to do wrong," replied Deacon Smith.

It was late that night when the owner of the brown cottage turned the key in her door. She was weary of body, but exultant of spirit. "Where on earth did this come from?" she asked aloud, unwrapping a big package which she had found on the step outside. In it was a beautiful winter coat, and the tag read, simply, *To Aunt Becky from her boys.*

The prayer ascending from the cottage that night concluded with, "Lord, I thank Thee that Thou as of old can still satisfy the soul's yearnings, so that youth is renewed like the eagle's. Old Becky doesn't want to be laid to rest just yet. If it be Thy will, she's ready for some more boys!"

CARRIE B. ILSEY *wrote for inspirational and family magazines during the first third of the twentieth century.*

FIVE

HE KNEW LINCOLN

Ninde Harris

Only a cub reporter, yet they were giving him the chance to cover a *big* story—a senator, two college presidents, a great minister—what an opportunity!

But then, the valve stopper on his mother's washing machine blew out and left his one good suit a soggy wreck.

What was he to do?

What he inadvertently discovered was that true heroes are found in the most unlikely places.

The dull thud of the electric washing machine wakened Jerry about ten o'clock. He turned over in his bed, muttering maledictions on all washing machines. He saw it was still early for a man who worked at night to rise. As he started to close his eyes again, he glanced at the calendar and saw that it was February 12, and he remembered that he was to cover the Lincoln Club's annual luncheon in honor of that great American.

With a leap he was out of bed, the covers thrown over its foot. He must hurry his bath, get dressed, and do some of his routine work at the *Star* office before he went to the luncheon. The speeches after it were sure to last until four o'clock. He wanted to hear all of them and get a good story for his paper. The evening papers had to go to press at two o'clock, so their stories could hit only the high spots.

This was his first big assignment. *Not such a bad assignment for a fellow who's been a cub reporter for only three months,* he told himself while he let the water into the tub for his morning plunge. *A senator, two college presidents, and a great minister to be among the speakers. Big meeting! Looks as if I'm making good with the* Star.

He whistled while he splashed water until his mother, reading carelessness in the sounds, came to the door and warned him not to get the clean window curtains wet.

Back to his room he went to don his best suit and new tie. The occasion demanded his best clothes. It was his big chance, as he saw it, to write a story which would inspire hundreds of the people in his town to a greater degree of patriotism. Jerry knew the city needed this. He hoped to arouse a civic pride that would demand that the school board build some new school buildings in the poorer quarters of town, rather than a million-dollar high school building on the east side where only the rich lived, and where only two hundred high school pupils would be enrolled for half a dozen years.

He told his mother about his plans while he ate his breakfast in the kitchen. She turned the current off the electric washer so she could hear him better. Because he worked until 2 A.M. and ate his breakfast alone, she had fixed a special little table in the kitchen. That hour was their time of visiting together.

"You know, Mom," he began, "if I make good with this story and get the raise I want, I'm hoping to have one of the basement rooms fixed up for a laundry and hire Mahala again, just as you used to have her before so many of us got into high school and college, and you had to begin doing without everything."

"Jerry," his mother came over and put her arms lovingly around his shoulders, "I'm not thinking of a laundry room and conveniences myself. I'm hoping this story of yours will move folks so they'll do what you want them to do about the schools in this town—replace those dilapidated ones on the west side and down by the river. We don't need that high school building to delight some rich real estate men who want it to make their subdivision grow. Perhaps you can help out by showing them how Lincoln rose from uneducated poor people."

She was going to tell him more about the school buildings when she noticed that in some mysterious way the valve stopper of her electric washer had dropped out, and a stream of soapy water was pouring onto the kitchen floor.

She started toward it to turn off the water, but Jerry was there before her. He caught the stopper from the floor, started to force it into the valve, and then his feet slipped. The next minute he was lying flat on the floor, the stream of water from the washer pouring onto his right shoulder and running down the inside of his coat.

Back on his feet again, Jerry and his mother laughed together, just as the Irish will in the face of accidents. But when both had sobered, and they could see the damage done to his clothes, her arms went close around him. "O Jerry boy, I'm so sorry! Now you'll have to wear your old suit to the banquet."

"Bother—I—" Jerry started and then stopped. Just a hint of big fear in his mother's eyes stopped him. He had been going to say that he couldn't possibly go to the banquet in his old clothes. He was going to impress her again with the standing of the men to be there, and give way to his own disappointment. But that look in her eyes stopped him in time. He resolved never to let her know what this accident would cost him.

So back upstairs he went to dress again. If he'd been a girl he would have cried, he concluded. As it was, he shut his teeth tight together and held his chin high. He'd go to the luncheon in patched trousers before he'd ever let his mother know just how deep his disappointment was.

But Jerry McGabe discovered a few minutes after he arrived at the office that he wasn't to go to the banquet at all. The city editor gave him a keen, searching glance as he, wearing his everyday suit, entered the office. "Guess you forgot the Lincoln Club banquet," he began. "Never mind, Jerry, you won't have time now to go home and dress for it. I'll send Bill Hawton. He's already dressed up as usual. You can take part of his beat—the fire houses and libraries. You may pick up some small stuff on them. Bill seldom does."

The city editor frowned severely at Bill, who merely ignored the look and began fussing at his tie.

Banquets and dinners were Bill's delight. They gave him a chance to be so dignified in appearance and impressive in bearing. He liked to sit close to the celebrities, and actually felt at times that he was one of them.

Jerry was bitterly disappointed. Why, this was worse than he had dreamed it would be. He had planned to go in his old clothes, get a back seat, and write the story anyway. He wanted to write it so that it would rouse all Lindendale's civic pride and sense of fairness in making improvements for the entire city and not just a part of it.

He decided to make some suggestions to Bill Hawton. He crossed over to him. "Thought perhaps there might be something in those speeches which we could localize and make relevant to the school board's building program," he began.

Bill looked at Jerry, whom he dubbed "the cub," with evident amusement. "Brother," he said, "that meeting and these speakers are too big to even think of the problems of this little burg, Lindendale. It's all about national problems. It's—"

But Jerry didn't hear the rest of Bill's remark, for the city editor called him to answer the telephone. An undertaker was calling to give a death notice, and who but the cub reporter would take small stories like that?

He ate his lunch at the regular thirty-cent counter across the street, and came back to the office to await more assignments. The editor soon had one ready. "You might stir around to some of the branch libraries," he said. "Get a list of the books most in demand at each one. The boss plans to use a little story on that each Sunday. Don't think it amounts to much myself, but the school superintendent is anxious to have him do it. And if there's anything Bill hates to do, it's to get those lists. He hasn't had one now for three weeks, and the boss is cross!"

So Jerry slipped into his overcoat again. He was positively sullen now. To hide the disappointment in his heart, he kicked the snow as he walked. He looked neither to the right nor to the left. When some boys at the Garretson school pelted him with snowballs, he didn't even turn to toss a few back at them. They opened their eyes wide and stood still and stared at each other. Jerry McCabe was usually a good fellow. Now he didn't even notice them. "Is he stuck up, or has he lost some of his pep?" they asked each other.

Jerry took down the names of the most popular books at that school branch library and started to hurry from the building. But the principal of the building sighted him. There had been an assembly, with speeches in honor of the day, and she wanted Jerry to take the program and write a story about it. Jerry took the program, but was wary in promising much of a story. For he knew the city editor had plenty of stories with lists of songs or accounts of speeches in them.

The next school he visited was the Altoons, one of three he and his mother had decided needed rebuilding. It was close to the river and very dilapidated. "Do the children read many books here?" he asked the librarian, who was a vivid little creature, just a girl in fact. "You'd think they would be too discouraged by this old building even to take books," he continued.

"Do they read?" she returned. "They certainly do—every book that comes to these shelves. They attend my story hours, too, and we have mothers' reading clubs. They're not the rich children who can stop school when their buildings are not to their liking. They come on, even when they have to raise umbrellas above their desks on rainy days.

"But if you want to see children with real zeal about reading and a librarian who's the wonder of the town," she smiled brightly, "go to the Cromwell school. It's the poorest building in the city, and the library has the largest circulation of any branch. We've tried to get reporters to write that one up, but they don't seem to think much of it." Her eyes brightened. "Oh, I believe you're a new reporter on this beat. I do hope you can get something in your paper about the libraries. That other fellow was so high and mighty, I was afraid to tell him the best places to get stories or help him with anything."

So Jerry went on to the Cromwell school building, built in the days of 1861. It had funny little windows; many chimneys telegraphed the story that it was heated by stoves; and it had a crowded, cindery school yard. He found that the library was in the basement of the dilapidated building, at the foot of a dark flight of stairs. Surprisingly, the room had cheerful curtains at the little windows, still more cheerful posters on the wall, and a little librarian who was charged with energy and interest in the work, and the little children, who filled the room almost to the overflowing point.

He discovered that she was telling a Lincoln story, and that she was too absorbed in it even to see him. He himself stepped into the shadow and soon forgot everything—the city editor, the grief he had felt because he would not see his name on the front page of tomorrow's paper—and was intently listening to the story she was telling. He heard her end it, and then say, "Now comes our beautiful Lincoln picture. We shall give it to Leonard Tuller this year, because the committee thinks that his hauling all the crippled children to school on his sled last winter made him the most deserving of all of you."

The children clapped their dirty little hands. They stood on tiptoe as Leonard, a thin little fellow, pushed through the crowd to get the picture. They stamped their feet, and they jumped up and down when he had taken it in his hands. And when he turned back toward them, Jerry saw his face, his eyes alight with joy and his whole face beaming with happiness. And high above his head, the little fellow held an expensive print of Abraham Lincoln, framed in a beautiful walnut frame.

Jerry didn't think of a story then. He wanted to shake Leonard's hand. And when he looked up, Jerry was directly in front of the little librarian.

"This is the tenth picture of Lincoln I have given to the Cromwell children," she told one of her women patrons. "Just think, I've been here for ten years. Grandfather bought the first three pictures for me. You see, Grandfather knew Lincoln, and he wanted me to inspire one boy each year to try to be as much like the great American as he could. He said that each boy so inspired, would leaven a whole bushel more."

Jerry knew right then that there in that room was a big Lincoln story—not about the grandfather who had known Lincoln, but about the librarian and the ten children who had learned Lincoln from the prints given to them during those ten years. He wondered if the librarian had all their names, and if he could find out from her where they were now and what they were doing.

He asked her if she had them. She nodded smilingly, and gave him all the names and present addresses. Three had left town. But she knew all about them—the boy who was still sick in a government hospital and who had won a French Cross overseas; the one who was assistant engineer for a construction company in South America; and the one who was a missionary in South Africa. They were the oldest of "her boys."

Jerry dropped in to see some of the others. Tom Morris, acting as assistant secretary to a boys' club while he went to high school, had hung his picture of Lincoln in the club gymnasium. "When I tell the boys of the wounded soldier whose proudest boast was that he knew Lincoln, they are fairer and squarer in their games," he said. "I think they feel they know him too."

Tim McCarthy's picture of Lincoln hung in his sick mother's room. Tim was having a hard time going to school and acting as nursemaid for her. "He gets these children to do their part of the work by telling them about Lincoln. It does seem that we all knew him, so naturally do we all talk about him now."

On and on Jerry visited the people who had "known" Lincoln. And from the west side of town he finally went back to the office of the *Star*. There Bill Hawton, back from the banquet, was talking pompously of the celebrities he had met. But Jerry hardly heard him.

He dropped the finished story into the city editor's copy basket as he went out to cover his beat, and didn't have time to think much about it until he was back at the office writing more short news items. Then the city editor came over to his desk. "Sent out and got a photograph of that librarian in your story," he said. "You weren't here, so I sent Miss Lilly."

Jerry's cheeks glowed. They sent out for photographs at the *Star* only when some story was particularly good. He was pleased, but he wasn't expecting the front-page spread that came in the first edition.

There was his story in the center of the front page, with his name signed in a very conspicuous way. On one side was a picture of Lincoln; on the other, one of the little teacher.

Later he thought to look for the story of the Lincoln Club luncheon. He looked a long time before he found it on an inside page, just three paragraphs long and placed in an inconspicuous corner.

He couldn't keep from walking up to the city editor. "I don't think I know the value of stories yet," he confessed. "I was bitterly disappointed to miss that Lincoln Club."

The man who had read stories and made up papers for ten years, and who had made many good feature writers in that time, shook his head. "That's not a real story at all," he explained. "Big stories are stories of accomplishment like this one. Why, son, this is the best story we've had this year! It's a real Lincoln story. That library teacher made those youngsters feel they really knew Lincoln. He's influencing that neighborhood as if he were alive. And you, with the heart throbs your story has in it, made me feel as if you had known him too.

"The boss agrees. He's writing an editorial on the work done by those schools in the poorer parts of town, and demanding that the board give them new buildings instead of building that useless million-dollar high school."

Jerry carried a stack of papers home under his arm. He woke

his mother to show them to her. "Mother," he began, "there will be a raise for me out of that story. You're to get every cent of it until you have that washroom fixed. Though I'm blessing that old washer for breaking when it did."

His mother sent him on to his room while she read the story and then the editorial, and quietly and thankfully she folded her hands. "With him writing that way, and thinking of me first of all when he gets a raise," she said softly, "it looks as if my boy was one of them that knew Lincoln."

NINDE HARRIS *wrote for inspirational and family magazines during the first half of the twentieth century.*

GERM-PROOF

Allison Ind

In the world of medical research, mistakes can be costly—indeed, they may be lethal. Vaccines, for instance. How terrible if they were incapable of delivering what they promised!

———

A sudden wave of apprehension and horror rendered Bugs Wells inanimate for one long instant; then he leaped. But he was too late.

He had been standing in the main bacteriology laboratory of Center Medical College, listening intently so that he should not miss a single word coming from the lips of one of science's greatest bacteriologists, Dr. Hartley Rock-Nestor, his chief. Uneasily Bugs's eyes had flashed now and then in the direction of the new Russian transfer student, Revelsky. Always a slovenly worker, Revelsky had been careless today.

Today, of all days, the class was working with the deadly germs of anthrax, or cattle blackleg.

"You know, Wells, lad, they're all wrong on their guess about this new sickle fever," Dr. Rock-Nestor was saying. The dean of laboratory workers was talking, he who had spent most of his life discovering death-producing germs and the rest of it in developing serums by which doctors could beat germs at their own deadly work.

"Sickle fever's new, and it's puzzling," he went on. "And because it's hit the country so suddenly, we've gone a bit panicky."

Bugs nodded. What can be more terrorizing than a disease that emerges out of the darkness and strikes people down before they recognize it or have a chance to fight back?

"Yes," he agreed. "That and the fact that the patient looks so bad with those queer sickle-shaped marks all over the body—high fever and alternate periods of coma and delirium."

Bugs was grave. This sudden onset of sickle fever, as mysterious and demoralizing as the recent outbreak of sleeping sickness, was making whole communities nervous, was filling emergency hospital wards and, alas, too frequently was taking the father from his tasks forever, the mother from her home, and the child from his crib. Household pets, too, were its victims. No serums had been developed yet to protect anyone from the terrible disease.

In the realm of science, workers new and veteran peered through their microscopes, scanned rows of glass test tubes in which were growing countless millions of germs, and studied with knitted brows men and beasts ill with the disease. Laboratory workers, too, became ill. Some died, their bodies showing the terrifying mark of the purple sickle.

"I tell you we're not going to find the organism by trying to grow it in test tubes," declared Dr. Rock-Nestor. "It is spread from insect to man, not from man to man. We must find the insect!"

Bugs cast another quick glance at Revelsky. How many times had he been shown the proper laboratory method of working with bacteria! The fellow simply would not learn.

"I understand that your old friend, Dr. Petroach, is going to try to prove before the Bacteriology Association convention here next week that the organism is a tiny rod-shaped germ," Bugs said nervously.

"He's wrong!" snapped Dr. Rock-Nestor. "Petroach and I have engaged in many scientific battles. Sometimes he's won; sometimes I have; but this time I shall stake my reputation on my contention."

"At the convention?" demanded Bugs. He had not heard of this. The very thought of that gathering of the nation's foremost bacteriologists brought a stab of pain to Bugs. Endless days and nights of painstaking research in the laboratory to prove his point regarding the typhoid bacillus; then something had gone wrong with the experiment. Frantically he had worked. Whatever was wrong stayed wrong—and thoughts of the Shilling Research Fellowship went glimmering in a sickening haze of defeat. No more funds. Already he was in debt. He could not remain in school any longer. He blinked his serious gray eyes rapidly. His lips tightened.

Suddenly his breath stopped. "Revelsky—!" Bugs leaped, but the damage was done.

Revelsky was staggering backward, his eyes fascinated by a bright forceps, the end of which was buried deep in his thumb. The forceps had been used to handle parts of glass slides on which living germs were placed for examination under the microscope.

"Was that forceps contaminated with anthrax?" demanded Bugs.

Dully Revelsky stared; then dully he nodded. Against all rules he had failed to sterilize the instrument after using it. Now it was buried in his thumb.

Bugs seized Revelsky's wrist. A quick motion and the forceps was extracted.

"Make it bleed!" barked Dr. Rock-Nestor. "Come. The hospital. They must have protective serum there to kill the anthrax germs he's introduced into his own bloodstream. Come!"

Dr. Rock-Nestor's big car flew over the highway. Staring, always staring before him, sat Revelsky, holding the infected thumb straight out.

The serum was his one hope.

Serum? Yes, the University hospital had a fresh stock. The quick pain of a hypodermic needle.

"You go back to the laboratory. I'll stay," was Dr. Rock-Nestor's order. Bugs walked back with his nerves tender and jumpy.

The class had been dismissed by the junior assistant, and the laboratory was in exact order except for Revelsky's instruments and apparatus. Methodically sterilizing every article except the growing cultures of anthrax, Bugs stowed the articles. Through the thin glass Petri dish in which organisms were grown by means of a special, transparent jelly-like food, Bugs stared at the thin filamentous colonies of living germs.

He shook his head, for scattered throughout those filamentous growths were others—colonies that did not belong there. Revelsky's careless workmanship had allowed contaminations to slip in—weeds growing with the grain. Unclean dishes or instruments might do that.

That night Bugs worked late in the laboratory, trying as never before to solve the puzzle of his persistent experiment failure. Too late he worked without anything to eat, for he went home with that old pain gnawing in his stomach. He was not feeling well, that was all.

The next day he was too dizzy to report for work. That day he heard about Revelsky. Old Hollis, the dispenser, told him.

"He's developed sickle fever!"

A lightning-like thrill shot through Bugs.

Bugs could not get his mind off Revelsky. Poor chap! That evening he went to see him. The picture was not pleasant. Dr. Rock-Nestor, haggard and weary, was constantly at the Russian's side. Bugs went back to the laboratory. Poor Revelsky! The serum had protected him against the anthrax in his own Petri dish, but not from the sickle fever.

Anthrax in the dish—sickle fever—anthrax—sickle fever—The thought crashed through.

Bugs leaped up, his pulse racing. Of course! From the refrigerator storage shelf he seized Revelsky's contaminated anthrax Petri dish. Marks remained in the jelly where Revelsky's instruments had prodded the anthrax colony to obtain germs for study.

The instrument, under Revelsky's inexpert guidance, had pushed right on through the anthrax colony into another colony, so thin and waterlike that he never would have seen it without special light. Whatever foreign germ was growing there had gotten on his instrument along with the anthrax. Probably both kinds of germs were on that forceps!

Now began to operate that uncompromising drive for truth that made Bugs stand out as one of the most promising of all Rock-Nestor's protégés. Nothing could stop him.

Swiftly he worked. His head swam. He must go home. In the hall he met Hollis. The old man was drooping.

"Why, Hollis! Why are you here so late?" Bugs asked anxiously.

The old man shook his head slowly. "It's King—you know, my dog," he muttered sadly. "Sickle fever."

"You mean—dead?"

Hollis nodded, blinking fast. The dog had been his only companion.

"I am *so* sorry," offered Bugs sincerely. "Where is he?"

"Upstairs."

Bugs patted the old dispenser's hand kindly; then turned to go. Instead, he raced off upstairs.

All the rest of the night he worked. Dawn found him sure, absolutely sure! From the dog dead of sickle fever Bugs had recovered certain germs—tiny spheres, *cocci,* bacteriologists called them—that moved furiously exactly as had those from Revelsky's culture. Certain other tests he would have to perform before science could accept his claims, but in his own heart he was sure. He had discovered the true germ of the baffling and dreaded sickle fever! That was one of the first steps in controlling any disease: identifying the germ that caused it.

Now he must make a preventive serum. Something that could be given folk so that they would be protected against the disease. Just like the preventives for smallpox, diphtheria, typhoid fever! Sure. That was the next step. End dreadful epidemics before they got started.

Bugs snatched three hours' sleep on the hard laboratory floor;

then he was at it again. He knew the method. He had made small-pox vaccine. All day he worked, and all that night, too.

Yes, Petroach was wrong; but just as surely as Bugs had proved him wrong had he proved his beloved Dr. Rock-Nestor wrong. Rock-Nestor was going to stake his reputation on his belief that the bite of infected insects was responsible for the disease in man. Bugs had found it different. Right here on the eve of his retirement from a career as beneficial to suffering humanity as it had been eventful and brilliant, Dr. Rock-Nestor was to be humiliated before an association of which he had once been president—by a young cub of an assistant. He was to be disproved instead of supported by the same intern he had loaned money to in pinched times, and had taken into his home, his laboratory, and in his gruff, but deeply sincere way, had looked on as a son.

Bugs buried his head in his hands. He had completed the sort of report that unquestionably would land any young worker the Shilling Fellowship. It would land it for him, and several years of advanced work, all expenses paid, would be his. He had done the work honestly. The results were in his hands, but that was not all—so was Dr. Rock-Nestor's reputation.

Wearily Bugs got up. Still more wearily he went home. He did not eat. He barely could sleep.

As he went back to the laboratory in the pale morning light, his face was gray and grim. Bugs was going to place Revelsky's Petri dish on Dr. Rock-Nestor's work table. The old scientist was sure to investigate those colonies.

Slowly he went across the hall. His key let him into the private laboratory of Dr. Rock-Nestor. He placed the Petri dish on the spotless work table and returned to his own laboratory.

The fire of research that had burned within him would not be quenched. Slowly, but with increasing energy, as the fire burned brighter again, he went to work to make a vaccine for sickle fever.

The fire leaped up now. He ignored all else, particularly the elaborate preparations being made to receive the convention. Deliberately he remained away from Dr. Rock-Nestor's laboratory.

The convention met, its hundreds of bacteriologists from all over the country listening to reports, criticizing, approving, refusing. Bugs did not attend the sessions. He felt that he could not.

He had another reason, though. He felt sick; really sick. It was the first afternoon of the convention that he sat languidly staring at the test tubes in which he had prepared his vaccine. He felt sure it was good; but to prove it he would have to test it on an animal exposed to the disease. If, after receiving a portion of the preventative, then exposed to the disease, the animal refused to become sick, he would know it was all right. Doctors could administer it.

His head ached so. His bones ached. He had a shooting pain up the back of his neck. "I won't be down tomorrow," was all Bugs said to old Hollis when he left the laboratory that evening, nor did he report the next day. He felt too weak. He felt better in bed—if only the bed would remain still.

Today was the day Dr. Rock-Nestor would be telling the convention all about the real causes of those purple sickles on the skin.

Sure—right there on his own arm they were. See them there? That was queer too. Someone must have put them there. It got too dark to see them. It was night.

The next day he saw them, though. Queer. Silly things. Why look at them? Just lie back in the funny bed, cool, quiet.

Really, it was not quiet now. He could hear voices. Dr. Rock-Nestor was telling Petroach and others about sickle fever. Yes sir. Telling all about it right there beside his silly, floating bed.

Why didn't Rock-Nestor leave him alone? Pinching his arm like that.

Everyone was gone. It was dark again.

Daylight came. Bugs' eyes blinked. The bed was quiet. The light was strong.

"Why—Doctor R-R-Rock-Nestor. You're here?" Bugs muttered.

The old scientist whirled on him. Two other men were there. They crowded close.

"Look!" cried Dr. Rock-Nestor.

"He's rational again. Getting better every second!" barked one of the others.

"It's proven!" thundered Dr. Rock-Nestor. "The vaccine against sickle fever is found! Do you hear, Petroach? It not only is protective, but actually kills the already established infection in humans!"

That stocky individual gripped Rock-Nestor's lean hands. "You win, sir. Proud to acknowledge it. You've saved him. Now go save others."

Once more Bugs had failed. If he had not been taken sick, at least he might have developed the vaccine completely.

The expression of supreme joy on Dr. Rock-Nestor's face fascinated him. In spite of himself, Bugs smiled feebly.

Petroach, splendid loser, noted the look too. "Rock-Nestor," he said. "I've heard it said that you'd rather have one of your students succeed than to succeed yourself. I can believe that now."

"Bosh!" barked the master. "Good work is good work. And who's to deny that he didn't do a splendid job in finding the germ and developing the vaccine?"

Bugs blinked stupidly. Were they talking about *him?* "I f-f-found it—?"

"Most certainly! Who else? Hollis told us you were sick. We

came and found you here." Rock-Nestor shook his head gravely. "But back in your laboratory, we found that vaccine you'd been making. I read your notes, Bugs. I found the whole story. You'd found that germ. But you'd gone farther. You'd developed a vaccine!"

"B-b-but the vaccine never has been tested. The convention never would accept it as proved," Bugs whispered.

Rock-Nestor glowered. "Is that so?" he snapped. "It's your own vaccine. And I used it to save your life. You were your own test animal. And you're germ-proof now. That's proof enough, isn't it, young man?"

Bugs was laughing silently now. Dr. Petroach approached. "You—you wouldn't care to work in my laboratory when you've recovered, would you?"

"Get on with you, sir!" growled Rock-Nestor. "The Shilling Fellow works right here in my own laboratory." The scientist fixed Bugs with his eagle eyes. "Doesn't he?" he demanded.

"A-a-address correct, sir," acknowledged Bugs.

ALLISON IND *wrote for inspirational and family magazines during the first half of the twentieth century.*

SEVEN

THE BIRD MAN

Mary Brownly

If ever I get discouraged or frustrated, all I have to do to remedy that is reread the story of this man's life, and note what *he* overcame. Studying Mary Brownly's life sketch of John James Audubon reveals to me new insights into the meaning of the word *hero*. So does the story of his indomitable wife, Lucy Bakewell Audubon.

———

Near the close of a long summer day a clerk, glancing idly from the window of the Relay Inn, one of Louisiana's picturesque taverns, saw a strange figure coming slowly down an old Indian trail leading out of the nearby woods.

"Look," he called to one of the loungers who sat in the office, "here comes the old man of the forest himself, but loaded with what?"

"Sticks, it appears."

"Well! Sticks I should say—no, it looks like a mountain eagle's nest and a leather pouch. I wonder where he's going? There are some queer men in the woods these days, but he is the oddest I have ever seen."

They watched a few minutes longer. "Why," exclaimed the clerk, "it looks as though the fellow were making for the tavern! What shall I do with him if he comes and asks for a room? The members of the circuit court are to sleep here tonight, and everything is taken."

The man came out of the forest, stepped up on the wide oak veranda, and laid the huge nest very carefully on the floor. He was not old, but his clothes were torn and dirty and his face wore a gaunt, hungry look.

"Hey, you, old fellow!" called the clerk. "Don't clutter up the floors with your trash. We are going to entertain a party here tonight, and want things to look clean. What are you going to do with that bird's cordwood anyway?"

"That, my friend," replied the stranger, "is the nest of a white eagle." He seemed to regard it as a treasure.

"Well, what of it?" exclaimed the clerk impatiently. "Why do you bring it here?"

"My dear friend, I beg your pardon, but that nest is very rare. I climbed two days to secure it, and risked my life to bring it down the cliffs unbroken. I would not displace a single stick for a doubloon, and it is just as I found it. My arms ache from carrying it so carefully. Can you show me to a room?"

"Surely you do not expect to take that bundle of sticks with you into a regular room?" questioned the clerk scornfully.

"Yes, of course!" answered the stranger, and added, "Young man, are you not a little rude to a traveler who comes to you for hospitality?"

"Well," he said ungraciously, "leave your sticks in the wood-shed, and I'll give you a room in the attic. That's the best I can do. The rest of the house is all engaged for tonight."

"But I *must* take the nest to my room!" insisted the stranger. "I

wish to paint it before anything happens to disarrange it—to paint it just as the eagle left it on the cliff. I periled my life to secure that nest, and I will not part with it."

The clerk stared. "I would not give a penny for that nest as kindling wood on a cold winter day!" he exclaimed. "What can such rotten rubbish be to you?"

"It is my life!" exclaimed the man. "Oh, you don't know! You can't see! What power taught the winged dwellers in the chambers of the air to build a nest like that?"

"I'm sure I don't know," muttered the clerk. "But since you *must* take it with you, let me carry it up to the sky room, so as not to litter up the stairs."

"*You* carry it! I would not trust you to *touch* it! You, in your present state of ignorance, know little of the wonders of a nest like that. Did you ever read the book of Job?"

"No. What's in it? Who wrote it?"

"What's in it? The hidden secrets of the universe. Who wrote it? Job. He saw behind nature—he had visions of the instincts of the universe!"

Picking up his treasured nest, the man started up the stairs, carefully picking his way. As they passed the rooms on the second floor, the clerk called attention to the clean sand-stoned floors and cautioned him to be careful; but just at that moment he stumbled, and part of the precious nest fell.

"Now you've done it!" exclaimed the clerk, angrily.

The stranger's eyes filled with tears. "I would not have had that happen for a fortune," he said.

"Yes, but think of me with this floor to clean again and the company already arriving," the clerk blustered. "There is your room at the top of the stairs. Go on up and get into it before something else happens!"

And the strange man of the woods climbed the last steep stairs, threw himself on the bed, and wept like a child.

Later the clerk was telling the landlord of his experience with this "crazy fool."

"What did he look like?" questioned the landlord.

"Sort of a hermit-wanderer," was the answer, "with a Frenchy face and long hair."

Honorable Judge Rich, the guest of honor in the court party, stood near and heard the story. Reaching over, he tapped the landlord on the arm. "How do you know it is not the great Audubon himself?" he asked.

And so it proved. The "old man" who had wept over the destruction of an eagle's nest sat in a place of honor beside Judge Rich at the banquet table that evening, while a chagrined clerk waited upon him and wished he had been more gracious to the unkempt stranger of the afternoon.

This incident will serve as a fitting introduction to John James Laforest Audubon—scientist, artist, and writer and nature lover first of all; a man to whom the works of the Creator were not mere commonplaces, but rare products of the Superhuman Power; a man whose knowledge of the great out-of-doors was unequaled in his day; a man with such artistic skill that his painting of a wild turkey was so lifelike that its domestic relatives advanced en masse as the canvas stood drying on the farmhouse veranda, determined to drive this intruder back to the swamp; a man whose written descriptions of American birds and animals are regarded as high authority among nature lovers of our own day.

He was born at Mandeville, near New Orleans, Louisiana, in 1780, and the identical house where this event took place is said to be still standing. At the age of ten years he went with his mother on a visit to Santo Domingo, where she met tragic death. Soon afterward his father returned to his home in Nantes, France, where John was placed in school. But education pursued within the confines of the walls was not at all to the boy's liking. He loved to roam the fields, and his stepmother, who was passionately fond of him, helped to foster this desire. Whenever his father was away from home, she packed a bountiful lunch and sent him out to wander as he wished.

The return of his father, however, meant another term of imprisonment in the classroom. Mathematics John cordially despised, but in drawing he excelled, and for two years had the privilege of studying under the masters of France, an opportunity which he took full advantage of.

This was the revolutionary period in his country. Napoleon's armies were sweeping out to conquer the world, and an older brother was an officer under the great general. But this did not concern the boy in the least. At last, his father, despairing that he would ever become interested in what he considered worthwhile things, sent him back to the United States when he was seventeen, to look after the family estate near Philadelphia, Pennsylvania.

The young naturalist found life in Mill Valley ideal. He fairly reveled in his beloved out-of-doors, drew to his heart's content, and as he was well supplied with money, and was a musician of ability, his society was much sought after all through the countryside. It was during these carefree years that he met Miss Lucy Bakewell, the daughter of a neighboring farmer, who afterward became his wife.

But just when prospects looked brightest, his father's agent in New York vanished with all the Audubon funds entrusted to his keeping, and John found himself suddenly penniless. Borrowing money to pay his passage, he returned to France. Here he received a cordial welcome from the home folks and remained with them one year.

During this time he sketched about two hundred French birds.

Never for a moment did he abandon the all-absorbing desire of reproducing nature fresh and lifelike as though just from the hand of its Creator.

His country was now about to enter upon a war with Europe, and offered a poor asylum to a young man who did not wish to fight. To avoid conscription he enlisted in the marine service, made one short voyage, and then took passage for America. The ship on which he sailed was overhauled by a pirate vessel on the high seas and he saved his gold only because he was fortunate in hiding it under the cable in the bow. Finally, however, he reached New York safely, and returned to his beloved woods with fresh ardor.

Despite his best endeavors, the birds he drew looked stiff and unnatural. He tried hanging them by a string tied to one foot, with the idea of showing every position, but the wings drooped loosely, and there was no look of life when he had finished. One day as he lay on his back under a tree watching some pewees, he tried to sketch them alive. But of course their movements were so rapid that he could not finish any pose. Then he shot several birds, and tried raising or lowering a wing or tail by a thread to get the proper lifelike position, but this wasn't satisfactory either.

Determined to solve the problem, he spent a whole month without drawing a stroke, thinking, thinking, thinking! As a result of this concentrated effort, he decided to make a manikin of mud and cork and wire. This also proved a failure.

One morning the household was surprised when the master arose before daybreak and rode away in haste. His destination was a nearby town. When the stores opened, he was the first customer.

Wire he bought of many different sizes, and hurried home. Without stopping for breakfast, he took his gun, set out for the woods, and shot the first kingfisher he saw. Carrying it to the house carefully by the bill, he mounted it on a piece of soft board, piercing the body with wire and fixing the wings and head with finer wires into a lifelike pose. Eureka! It was done! And now Audubon began a series of illustrations which afterward formed a part of his great book, *Birds of America.*

In trying to do perfect work, his life purpose grew, and it should be noted in passing that he never took the life of a wild creature save as it was necessary in the interests of science.

Young Audubon was now anxious to marry the lady of his choice. But her father saw no substantial support in store for her, and demanded that his son-in-law-to-be turn his attention to some reasonably paying commercial pursuit. He even lent his assistance by securing him a position in a counting house in New York. But the young man pined away in the city environment, and spent his spare time, and some he should not have spared, in preparing specimens of stuffed birds. This became so obnoxious to the neighbors near his lodgings that they finally appealed to the police for "cessation of this nuisance," and at last he went home, poorer by $8,000, which sum he had invested in a business which failed.

But the new country of the great Central West was just opening up, and a future there looked so inviting that the stern father relented. Audubon sold his Pennsylvania farm, and the young people started on their wedding trip in 1808.

It was an eventful journey. The stage in which they took passage for Pittsburgh was wrecked, and the bride was severely injured. For twelve days they floated down the Ohio River on a flat-bottom boat, at last reaching Louisville where, in partnership with a friend, the naturalist started a store.

Here Alexander White visited him as a stranger, and tried to interest him in a book of bird drawings which he himself was contemplating publishing. Audubon brought out his portfolios and generously offered the use of his own pictures for the giving of the author's name. Mr. White, however, did not avail himself of this privilege.

Whoever heard of an artist making a success in commerce! Audubon's partner was none too honest, the business failed, and he moved his family to Henderson for the purpose of making a new and, he earnestly hoped, more successful venture. But before settling down to any routine, he decided to take a trip down the Mississippi River as far as Sainte Genevieve in Missouri. Mishaps beset the party from the start, and finally they were snowbound near an Indian camp for several weeks. While his companions fretted and fumed at the hardships and delay, Audubon cheerfully ate the pecans and wild turkey meat which were their only food, and enjoyed to the full this association with the wild men and animals of the new country.

Returning to his family, he seems to have taken life seriously for seven years, for he bought some land and a number of slaves, and was very happy in his home. Here Daniel Boone, that "prince of hunters," visited him, and also the picturesque Rafinesque.

This last-named individual was an eccentric old naturalist who went into ecstasies of delight when Audubon showed him a new specimen of plant. The visitor was told he could sleep in the spare room—a loft chamber—and in the night his host was awakened by a most unearthly racket coming from that quarter. Hastening to the rescue, he found the old man rushing madly about trying to kill a host of bats which were flying about overhead. His weapon was Audubon's rare Cremona (one of the most valuable violins in the world). Only the handle was left. The violin itself was smashed to splinters. Rafinesque, it seems, thought that these animals were "a new species," and forgot everything else in his anxiety to capture a specimen.

But once more the wanderlust claimed its own, and Audubon, when he left home, packed over two hundred drawings in a stout wooden box and stored them in the house of a friend. Returning, he found that a pair of Norway rats had reared a family among the bits of paper that a few months before represented over one thousand inhabitants of the air. At first he was actually sick with disappointment, but in a few days, consoling himself with the thought, *I can do them better now,* he went to work, and within three years had again filled his portfolios.

About this time his father died, and John generously relinquished all claim to the estate, taking only $17,000 which came to him in cash. This he invested in a business which failed before he had realized one dollar of profit.

Taking all he possessed—his sick wife, his gun, his dog, and his precious drawings—he returned to Louisville, and in order to keep the wolf of hunger from the door, began doing portraits in crayon. Through all these changes of fortune his wife's courage never failed. "With her I am always rich," her husband declared.

Starting on a tour of the Southern states to study birds, Audubon's stay lengthened to fourteen months, and he returned to find his family settled at Bayou Sara, near New Orleans, where his wife had opened a school for young ladies, specializing in music and French. From this time on he devoted himself exclusively to ornithological work. People called him a lunatic and a fool, but still he persevered, assisted by his two sons, Victor and John.

In 1824 he went to Philadelphia to exhibit drawings which he hoped to publish. Not only cold water, but ice water was thrown upon his project. He was so poor at this time that his biographer states he could not pay the trifling toll over the bridge to Goat Island when he visited Niagara Falls on his return journey. His devoted wife, however, about this time came into an inheritance which yielded her an income of $3,000 a year. All this she gladly turned over to her husband, enabling him to continue his work and make a trip to England, where he was received kindly and greatly encouraged.

For the next twelve years Audubon virtually lived in the woods, journeying thousands of miles, with his unerring rifle killing only to embalm the wild creatures by an art of his own which preserved them unchangeable in form and coloring. Always he kept in mind the book he meant to publish.

Finally, he found an engraver in England to do his work, but he was of necessity his own publisher.

In 1827 the prospectus for *Birds of America* was ready, and the author, acting as his own agent, went out into a strange country to secure subscribers. It was planned to issue the work in ninety numbers of five plates each, and Audobon had no money to pay for the first number. There were to be in all 448 plates, containing more than a thousand life-size bird figures. The edition was to cost $100,000 to publish [a vast sum even in today's money].

But Audubon's work had already attracted wide attention in Europe, and finally he secured the necessary subscriptions from men of wealth.

An exhibit of his pictures at the Paris Academy of Sciences attracted much notice, and Gerard called him "the King of Ornithological Painters."

After spending some years in England, Audubon came home to America in 1839, buying an estate on the banks of the Hudson in New York, where he set about the preparation of a cheaper edition of his book, which would be within reach of the poorer people.

Audubon's life had been a strenuous one, but still a love of the wild burned in his heart, and he started on a last journey, bound for the Far West, then just opening up. Almost within sight of the Rockies, he was obliged to turn back because of feebleness. Three years more he lived, and failing eyesight accomplished that which hardship could not do—it broke his spirit. At last he became totally blind, and his death occurred January 27, 1851.

His great book is now very valuable and rare, the plates having been destroyed by fire. Today, surviving copies bring a fortune whenever one is offered at auction.

MARY BROWNLY *was a well-known writer who specialized in biography during the first half of the twentieth century.*

EIGHT

HERO IN FEATHERS

Ella A. Duncan

How little we know of the inner worlds of the rest of God's creation! We know only enough to marvel and wonder. With what wondrous qualities our Lord endowed even the lowliest of His creatures. Even a duck named Waddles.

———

When the doorbell rang that spring morning, two-year-old Susie found a small duck nestled in a basket on the front step. It was just a round, yellow ball of fluff with two black, shiny beads for eyes and a curious ebony bill that went poking about constantly into everything. It had always seemed extremely cruel to give children such small, helpless beings; too many such defenseless creatures are tortured to slow death. Surely Susie would be no exception among children. John declared emphatically that the bit of down would be nothing but a nuisance; it was to be taken to the pet shop the next morning.

Then came the ordeal of separating one small, unreasoning being from another. From the moment she found him, all of Susie's other interests had been discarded for the tiny bit of quacking life.

She was ecstatic when the duckling scrambled from his basket and waddled at her heels about the room. I tried to explain that he was just a baby duck and must go to his mother, but when I put him in a box on the back porch, Susie's howls from the front porch, and the duck's clatter, rent the air. We had to relent, but, of course, only temporarily.

Surprisingly, the little girl was gentle with the soft, fragile body of the duckling. As for him, from the very beginning there was no one else in the house but Susie. When she walked, he waddled at her heels; when she ran, he rolled over and over like an animated yellow tumbleweed, trying to keep up with her, and protesting such speed in high, hysterical quackings.

Susie spent hours, that first day, showing the birdlet her possessions. As the little girl displayed storybooks and blocks, the small duck nestled by her side, quacking contentedly. In her eagerness to make him understand, she bent her head to his level, chattering earnestly. In response, the yellow neck would stretch up and the beady eyes sparkle while the little duck talked in his own baby language. I have always thought that there is some canny or uncanny understanding between the young of the earth, something sadly impossible between adult animals. Watching the little blonde girl and the baby duck, I was sure that there was not only a sort of spiritual blending, but also a definite mutual understanding of language. There was no doubt of it in the weeks and months that followed.

Within the first hour Susie named the duck. She chose "Waddles," truly an appropriate name for an embryo hero—but I anticipate.

It was raining the next morning, so it was easy to grant Waddles a day of reprieve. I think we knew then that he would

never see the inside of a pet shop. Each morning after that we made feeble excuses for not sending him, until finally John exclaimed over his coffee, "Let's keep the little fellow. It would break Susie's heart to take him away now. Besides, I sort of like him myself," he finished sheepishly.

At last Susie had a playmate—her first. There being no children her own age near us, she had been alone among adults all her short months on earth. There had been no name in Waddles's basket, so we never knew where he came from. I am sure, however, some friend much older and wiser than we must have brought him—someone who knew that everything on earth longs for something its own age, something with which to share like experiences and joys. To Susie and Waddles everything on earth was still shiny new and wonderful beyond belief—things for exploring and exclaiming.

Together that summer in the high-fenced backyard, daughter and duck found a complete world of magic. To Ann, the maid, and to me, it was amazing how that funny little duck so quickly and completely took over what at times had been a real task for two adult human beings. The two chased butterflies, built castles in the sandbox, played hide-and-seek among the shrubs and lawn furniture, or just sat in the sun and chattered about things beyond the ken of a grownup world. There were hilarious games of their own invention, over which Susie went into spasms of laughter and Waddles quacked his glee in a voice that began to "change" as the summer wore on. His yellow down had given way to a thick coat of slate-gray feathers, marked with black. Because we knew nothing of his ancestry, we had no way of knowing what his breed line might be. He grew to be larger than most ducks, however, and was a strong, handsome fellow as he waddled proudly about the yard, head and shoulders held high.

Waddles had been with us two years when Baby Carol came, and Susie was ready for nursery school. We brought the baby home from the hospital in her bassinet, and Ann went to call the two playmates from the backyard. They stood silently, side by side, for a few seconds, studying the new red mite.

"Where are her teeth?" Susie wanted to know. But it was Waddles that surprised us most. Except for his various degrees of quacking, he had never made any other sound. Now he suddenly beat his great wings against his sides, let out a trumpeting honk, and sat down purposefully beside the bassinet. We did not know it then, but with that wild, foreign cry, Waddles was proclaiming to the world that he was at last an adult. On his shoulders had descended the grave responsibility of guard for a new, helpless being.

It was amusing, at first, to see the big duck there beside the bassinet, his neck held stiff and high, his keen black eyes darting in search of danger. Worn out from play with Susie, he had usually gone willingly to his box on the back porch. That night John had to pick him up and carry him—protesting and hissing—outside.

Early the next morning Waddles was at the back door, quacking urgently to be let in. After breakfast, to get rid of his infernal noise, I sent Susie out to play with him. Soon she was back. "He won't play with me any more!" she wailed.

"It's the truth," said Ann. "He just ignored her." I was torn with sympathy for my eldest daughter in this first tragedy of life, and she was utterly bewildered by it. But before the week was over, a little boy and a little girl, near her age, moved into the neighborhood. Then came the glorious experience of nursery school—and Susie was no longer a baby.

As for Waddles, it finally seeped through his small duck brain that the only time his guarding act was necessary was when Baby Carol was put in the backyard for her sun bath. The rest of the day he waddled majestically about the yard, muttering philosophically to himself, or sat in the sun and brooded contentedly. The only time he resembled his former animated self was when the time for the sun bath drew near. He was always at the back door waiting. If Ann or I were late getting her out, he set up a demanding clatter. In a restrained frenzy of excitement, he would waddle beside the carriage until it was stopped. Then, always facing the house, he settled beneath it, every inch of his body at trained attention.

Once more, I was having reason to give thanks for Waddles as an aid to child rearing. It was impossible to teach Susie and her newfound friends to close the back gate as they should, but as long as Waddles was around, neither man nor beast could come near his baby. The dogs and cats of the neighborhood soon learned to avoid that gate. Even the milkman asked if he might leave the milk at the front each morning, rather than battle the big duck.

It was Waddles himself I worried about at first. I was afraid he might get out and wander off, or be run over in the street. After the second venture up the driveway to the front of the house, however, he evidently decided that the outside world held little of interest for him. He returned to his big backyard and never again left it. It was his kingdom, and woe betide the trespasser!

It was that very vigilance, however, that nearly caused his banishment; I shudder yet to think how very near we came to disposing of him.

Because of an illness, Ann had to leave us, and a new girl was employed in her place. The first morning that she took the baby outside, Waddles flew at her in a veritable fury of beating wings, snapping beak and clawing web feet. Before I could come to the rescue he had ruined the girl's hose and left her legs bruised and bleeding. In shock and anger, she quit. Two others followed in quick succession. It was impossible for them to avoid the backyard entirely. It was even more impossible to convince Waddles that they were to become a part of the family. Up until then, he seemed to have had an uncanny instinct for doing as he should. We had never punished him, and I had no idea how to go about it now. The only solution seemed to be exile.

Then—miracle of miracles—Ann came back. All was peace in

the backyard once again. I was not only thankful for that, and for her help, but a plague of rabies had broken out among the dogs of the town. Ann would guard the children as no strange girl could be expected to do, but we mothers lived in a nightmare of dread. We tried to cooperate in keeping the youngsters entertained, but it was difficult to restrain them.

One morning when there was no school, I had all the youngsters for a morning picnic. After the picnic Ann herded them into the house to get them ready for the moving pictures we were going to show. I took Baby Carol to the backyard for her belated nap. Making sure that the gate was closed, and Waddles settled in his usual fighting stance beneath the carriage, I went back into the house. The phone rang. A friend down the street said, "I just saw a dog turn into your driveway, and if I know a mad dog, that one is."

Every time a stray dog had been seen in the neighborhood for weeks, everyone was sure it had rabies. Nevertheless, prickles of fright were breaking out along my spine. Then I thought, *The back gate*—one of the children might have gone back for something. On legs that threatened to buckle, I started for the yard. Before I was halfway through the house, for the second time in his life came that high, wild honk...and I *knew!*

Screaming for Ann, I burst through the back door upon a scene that will remain with me the rest of my days. Not three yards from the baby was a misshapen, shaggy dog with a swollen head, red, unfocused eyes, and dripping mouth. Flying to meet him was Waddles, wings outspread and neck stretched forth, ebony beak snapping and cracking like a small, angry machine gun. I knew that Ann was close behind me with the broom; then I lost sight of everything, except the desire to gather my baby in my arms and race for safety.

Somehow I made it, with Ann and her broom as flanking

support. She slammed the back door behind us and ran to call the police. Too weak and paralyzed with fear to move, I leaned against the closed door and listened to the uncanny battle outside. The blood-chilling growls and muttered barks of the mad dog told me that Waddles was doing his best, but I knew that his best was not going to be enough this time. I was too frightened to look, but from the sounds coming through the opened windows, the shaggy dog and the big duck were fighting all over the backyard. Their bodies bumped and threshed against the side of the house and porch; then, except for the slapping of Waddles's big wings, the snapping of his beak and the duller sound of the dog's jaws, the fight would dim out. Waddles's first squawk of pain brought me to with the frenzied urge to do something.

"I can't just let him stay out there and fight alone when he doesn't have a chance!" I told Ann desperately.

"You certainly can't go out there and fight that mad dog bare-handed. Think of the children," she declared.

There was not a gun in the house, and the police could not possibly get there in time. I prayed that Waddles would somehow realize his danger and fly up on something out of reach before it was too late. But all the time I knew he would not. His stout little heart simply would not let him stop fighting until his enemy was driven from that yard. This time, however, his opponent lacked sense enough to flee, no matter what the punishment.

The pain-filled squawks and barks gradually lessened, as did the sound of the fight, until once again, all was quiet in the back-yard. It was an ominous, deadly quiet, and through it Ann and I clung together until the police came.

There was a muffled shot in the back, then one of the officers came to the door. "I want you to see a sight you will never see again," he said.

The backyard was a shambles. Chairs had been upset. Flowers and shrubs were beaten down. Baby Carol's carriage had been over-turned, and crisscrossing the sandbox, that had once held so much happiness for a small blonde girl and a little duck, were dark red stains. In the open gateway, a wing tip touching the fence on either side, lay Waddles—his broken neck outstretched and ebony beak turned scarlet. Just beyond him, in the driveway, lay the body of the great yellow dog.

"I don't think the bullet was necessary," said the second officer, still absent-mindedly holding his gun and looking with wonder at the mutilated head of the dog.

Somehow Waddles had managed to hold out, until he drove his last enemy from the little plot of earth he held sacred and dear above all other. Some inborn instinct from his wild, dim past must have warned him that this mad invader meant death and destruc-tion to everything he loved, and, like heroes the world over, he gave his life to preserve his little world and the happy way of life within it.

There were no medals or citations for Waddles—only a small grave in the corner of the yard he loved so well, and the deep, undying devotion in the human hearts that knew him.

ELLA A. DUNCAN *wrote for magazines during the mid-twentieth century.*

NINE

A NEW CELEBRATION
OF MEMORIAL DAY

Margaret W. Beardsley

Teacher Persis Clark felt that, for some unknown reason, her previous Memorial Day celebrations had fallen flat. What could she do this year to change the ho-hum into excitement?

Then came her inspiration.

And afterward: The message on the blackboard.

I took especial care in selecting a program suited to the day, both years I have been here," said Miss Clark, "and I didn't succeed in arousing an atom of enthusiasm either time. Indeed, Mr. Washburne, I'd be afraid to name a half dozen in the room who have any idea of what Memorial Day means beyond the vacation it brings."

There was a trace of indulgence in the principal's smile, as he waited for Miss Clark to continue. She was a good teacher. There was no other, perhaps, as good in the Graydon schools, but she was just a trifle intense on some subjects. Memorial Day might be one of them.

"I wanted to ask you why I have so dismally failed to get the spirit of the time. The day ought to mean something. If it doesn't, exercises of commemoration are surely better left alone." The principal's smile and its meaning were not lost on the underteacher, yet she went on: "I don't feel that I can humiliate myself by a repetition of the farce of the past two years."

Professor Washburne raised his eyebrows. "My dear Miss Clark, surely you're not suggesting that we abandon the exercises! We'd have the whole Grand Army down on us. As for your programs these preceding years, I can think of nothing to criticize in them. According to my memory, they were wisely chosen, and well carried out—very well, I should say; but if they haven't proved satisfactory to you, suppose you try something different."

"Anything I please?"

"*Anything,*" assented the principal, cheerfully, and turned to his desk.

All the way home, Persis Clark was saying over to herself, *I must think of something—something that will make them understand.*

That plural pronoun was sufficiently clear to herself. Her theys, theirs, and thems always meant the roomful of rollicking, mischievous, but loving—Persis knew that—girls and boys. She had reached no conclusion yet, when, after supper, she brought out two portraits. She was likely to get these out when perplexed. They were unfailing helps over hard places. One was a soldier, strong and handsome, and the other a white-haired, frail old man. The glow of pride in the gallant soldier softened to tender reverence as she studied the face of the latter portrait.

This was the face she had known, and she felt the smile in the eyes. She remembered just how the stool must be placed, so that he might stroke her head where it rested against his "well knee"; and the sound of his voice, softly modulated for her own especial hearing, was still in her ears. She had asked most often for stories of her soldier picture—and just then came Miss Clark's inspiration.

"Teacher's a-goin' to tell us something nice," whispered Dickie Hall to his seat mate next morning. Others had spied an anticipated pleasure in Miss Clark's face, and there was a small fever of excitement by the time the last gong had sounded.

"Next Friday," said Miss Clark, "will be Memorial Day, and I've been planning something for our Thursday afternoon exercises."

There was no mistaking the dismal falling off of interest in her listeners, but Miss Clark was undaunted. "I am thinking that instead of remembering these brave ones collectively, as we have done, this year we will be a little selfish, perhaps, and think and talk of those who belonged just to us. I mean those who were our relatives or dear friends of our families. I'll not ask for the names of your heroes yet. Think of it, and talk it over at home this noon and evening, and tomorrow morning we'll begin to write their names in the two scrolls on the front board. In one we'll place the names of soldiers buried in Graydon cemetery, and in the other those buried elsewhere.

"Now about our exercises for Thursday afternoon. I want each of you to be prepared with some story of your own soldier hero, and we'll tell these stories, and sing our national songs."

"And don't we have to get poems?" broke in Archie MacClain.

"Not a poem, Archie," declared Miss Clark, and the room echoed with relieved sighs.

"On Friday morning we'll meet here and go together to the cemetery to decorate our soldiers' graves there, so I wish you to take great care in getting stories of our other heroes, for those who are buried far away from friends—perhaps no one even knows where—ought to have especial remembrance on Memorial Day."

At recess the space round Miss Clark's desk was crowded. And that evening she was detained so long that she was surprised to find one of her pupils still lingering on the steps.

"Not gone yet, Frances?" she inquired. "Why, I believe you were waiting for me."

"I wanted to tell you," said the child, with the swift directness of a reserved nature, "that my grandfather, Francis Key Lane, is buried here at Graydon. He was a soldier, and I'd love to have him remembered, only I was afraid I couldn't tell you in front of the rest."

Miss Clark only said, "I will write his name first thing in the morning, Frances."

The words had brought to mind a chivalrous, old-school gentleman, standing with hat in hand while she spoke with his granddaughter. Persis remembered now that she hadn't seen them together since the last long vacation.

Frances was one of the teacher's "responsibilities." She was too quiet and reserved. She needed the "chummy" companionship of her mates. Whether her association always with older people had been a bar to childish comradeship, or whether the reserve was in accord with the mother's desire, Persis couldn't decide. She'd wished to meet Mrs. Westing, but had found her busy whenever she called. Perhaps this interest in common might bring her closer to her classmates.

Graydon had never known such a research in family history as that of the next few days; and in connection with the study of family heroes, the nation's history advanced suddenly from a stupid textbook to a par with the most delightful story any had ever read. All the older members of families with representatives in Room E were forced into constant reminiscences; chance visitors did not escape either; and never had old veterans been delighted with larger or more appreciative audiences.

There was a single exception to this general thirst for information. On Wednesday afternoon, Frances had not yet mentioned Thursday's exercises at home. Her mother and herself, besides the maid of all work, made up the household; and it had been one of those times when Frances saw her mother only at very silent mealtimes, followed by days when the typewriter clicked ceaselessly.

Frances listened as she came in from school. There was no sound of the busy little clicker, and she turned the knob of her mother's door softly. Three or four heavy envelopes lay stamped for the evening mail, and Mrs. Westing sat in an easy chair without even a tablet in sight.

"You are all through?" The wistful hope in the inquiry brought a pang to the mother's heart.

"All through," she answered, drawing the child into her arms. "Poor, lonely, neglected little daughter! Doesn't she know that mother would give her more time if she could?"

A swift kiss was an instant denial of neglect. "But, O mother, if only you could take time to come to the exercises tomorrow," and Miss Clark would never have recognized the shy Frances in her eager description of what these exercises were to be. "There are the names of soldiers in Cuba and the Philippines and in France, but those Miss Clark wants us to remember especially are those who fought in the Civil War; and, Mother, I know you'd love to see how beautiful Grandfather's name looks at the very top of the scroll. I can hardly tell which story to tell about him! It will do you good to come—" Frances broke off like the snap of a thread. There was such a strange look on Mother's face.

"If you had only risked bothering me, dear," said her mother after a moment, "it would have been better than putting Grandfather in a false light. They wouldn't want him with their heroes, Francie. I cannot understand how it came you didn't know, didn't learn from his stories, that Grandfather was a Confederate soldier."

"I never knew—I don't think Grandfather ever said," faltered Frances, crushed by the magnitude of her mistake.

Neither of them could know that Grandfather, with the chivalry of that highest type of knighthood—a gentleman—had carefully avoided in his stories anything bringing in a question of sides. He deemed this a courtesy due to the child's dead father, and the people among whom she lived, that her mind should not be prejudiced with the knowledge that he and they had once been enemies.

There was, perhaps, more bitterness than Mrs. Westing knew conveyed in her words. The world seemed hard at that moment. Some manuscript she had hoped much from had come back that afternoon, being "not exactly in the line required by our magazine at present," and now this Memorial celebration seemed like an intended humiliation of those she knew to have been brave and truehearted. But, because she was the daughter of her father, and because she had chosen her heart's dearest from among these people, she felt she ought not speak out to his child in passionate defense of their side—her father's and hers.

"Mother," said Frances, presently, "I think I'll let Miss Clark know tonight, and if you don't mind, I'll not go to school to-morrow."

"Let me send a note to your teacher," urged Mrs. Westing.

"Oh, no," cried Frances, "you've been writing all day." She couldn't thrust the responsibility of her mistake upon anyone else, but the word "note" was a boon to the sensitive child.

Mrs. Flanigan, the janitor's wife, vigorously swishing her broom in the lower hall, was startled some minutes later, by a hand on her arm and a "Will you please let me into Room E for a moment?"

"And phat are yees wantin' in Room E? Was it yer book ye wad be leavin'?" demanded the janitress. "For it's left till mornin' it is, then. It's meself's hed throuble enough wid other folks' leavin's bein' tuck."

"I don't want to take anything," assured Frances. "I just want to write something on the board to Miss Clark."

"An' yees wadn't be blackguardin' yer teacher in it?"

Frances had too indistinct an idea of the question's meaning to answer by a plain negative.

"I don't think I can come to school tomorrow, and it's something that Miss Clark must know."

"It's in bed yees oughter be this minute," declared Mrs. Flanigan, taking note of the child's pale face. "Sure an' I can't see the hairm, ef ye signs yer name."

And this was the message that Miss Clark read the next morning:

Dear Miss Clark:

Will you please take Grandfather's name off the scroll, and tell the flower committee they needn't make a wreath for his grave? I made a mistake. He was a soldier, but he was on the other side.

I'm sorry I didn't know [here a change of writing indicated a pause], but I can't be sorry about Grandfather. I know he was a brave soldier; and he never would have fought for anything he didn't think right. I believe I might have thought as he did myself. Please excuse my not coming to school.

Frances Lane Westing

"Children," said Miss Clark, when they were all seated that morning, "I wouldn't want you to feel that I had taught you to see only one side, or to be unforgiving and unloving at Memorial time. When we think of heroes, we should remember that on the other side there were men who fought bravely, giving up their lives willingly, who had brothers and sisters and little children to cherish their memories just as our brave ones had."

With hearts throbbing in the pride of their own heroes, the children listened to the strong plea that followed for the heroes of the "lost cause"; and when at last their teacher moved the screen, and read the pitiful little message from Frances, not one boy in the room pretended to have a stray eyelash, or cared who saw tears on his cheek.

There was a wildly unanimous standing vote to place flowers on the Confederate's grave, some almost mounting the benches in their enthusiasm, and one loud whisper proposing, "A yard deep."

Miss Clark, however, thought it might be well to get an expression from the parents, perhaps from the veterans, on the subject. If they had scruples, they should be allowed to express them before rather than after. She didn't think that there could be any objection to a quiet placing of flowers.

At dinner that day, Ruth Clayton asked her grandfather, excitedly: "Would you decorate a Confederate soldier's grave?"

The Judge looked at her seriously. "My dear little girl," he said, "there was one Confederate—I think it's unlikely he's still alive—whose grave I would walk many miles to cover with flowers, and stand by with uncovered head. I cannot expect to have this privilege. Our opportunities of strewing flowers on Confederate graves are not frequent; but in memory for the soldier who saved your grandfather, Ruth, I'd advise you never to miss one of them."

There was a clamor for a story not yet known, and the Judge placed his glasses on his folded paper, and related the following incident.

"I was very young when I went to war; much too young to endure long marches," he said. "It was one of those engagements, not noted in history, when our men fell back for a time. I was never hit with a bullet in battle, but that day's sun in our eyes was as fatal as shot to many. I was confused by the order to retreat. I remember only the order to fall back, and suppose I stumbled in the spot most exposed to the sun's rays. I came to consciousness later with the knowledge that water dripped on my face. I still have in memory a confused vision of a gray-coated soldier, though I think I didn't open my eyes much. I was lifted not long after in strong, careful arms, and gently carried some distance into what seemed a heaven in its comfort of shade, though it was only some bushes by a small brook. I felt him lift my hand and actually place it in the welcome cool water.

"Afterward I heard him say: 'Aid and comfort to an enemy—if this be treason, I reckon it will have to be so. I certainly can't be a traitor to Francis Key Lane.'

"I kept repeating these words long after I was left alone—not aloud, but to myself, as one does sometimes in a half-conscious state. I must finally have slept, and was awakened toward evening by a 'Hello, boy!' and found one of our own men with a pail in his hand, looking down at me. It had been but a few hours falling back for our men, and that Confederate must have risked something more than a charge of treason in his care of me."

Only Ruth's mother had observed her clap both hands to her mouth at the latter end of the narrative in a frantic struggle to keep from interrupting.

"Grandfather Clayton!" she burst out at his last word, "that's our Confederate!" and then Ruth became the storyteller, and her grandfather the excited listener.

The Claytons never wasted time. When the maid brought in

the dessert, there was no one left at the table. The family were assisting the Judge to find his hat, that he might lose no time in assuring himself of the strange coincidence between his own and Ruth's stories.

Never, never, had there been such a glorious commemoration of Memorial Day in the Graydon school as that held that afternoon in Room E. The children told their stories as bravely as their heroes had fought; and both the tales and their relators were vigorously applauded.

The Judge was there, and Mrs. Westing and Frances; for there had been no question of identity. It had been the very story most loved by Frances, and the Judge told it himself, to the delight of the school, while Ruth held Frances' hand and kissed her tenderly at the ending, when the boys cheered.

But the best time was next morning, when Graydon's Grand Army Post, led by its honored commander, Judge Clayton, halted at his command, and stood with uncovered heads while Room E heaped flowers—not a foot deep, but into a beautiful mound—over the Confederate's grave. And the widow knew at that moment that she and her child were finally accepted by the community at last and would nevermore be "strangers in a strange land."

MARGARET W. BEARDSLEY *wrote for inspirational and family magazines during the first half of the twentieth century.*

COALS OF FIRE

Author Unknown

Guy Morgan was angry. Dick Osgood had insulted him: called him a coward because he refused to fight. Now he wanted his mother to release him from his promise not to.

But she, remembering someone else, did not release him.

———————

Guy Morgan came in with rapid step and an impetuous manner. His mother looked up from her work. There was a round, red spot on his cheek, and an ominous glitter in his eyes. She knew the signs. His naturally fierce temper had been stirred in some way to a heat that had kindled his whole nature. He threw down his cap, collapsed on an ottoman at her feet, and then said, with a little of the heat of his temper in his tone, "Never say, after this, that I don't love you, Mother."

"I think I never did say so," she answered gently, as she passed her hand over the tawny locks and brushed them away from the flushed brow. "But what special thing have you done to prove your love for me just now?"

"Taken a blow without returning it."

She bent over and kissed her boy. He was fifteen years old, a great, tall fellow with muscles like steel; but he had not grown beyond liking his mother's kisses. Then she said softly, "Tell me all about it, Guy."

"Oh, it was Dick Osgood! You know what a mean fellow he is anyhow. He had been tormenting some of the younger boys till I couldn't stand it any longer. They are every one afraid for their lives when he's near them. I told him he ought to be ashamed of himself, and tried to make him leave off, till, after a while, he turned from them and coming to me, struck me in the face. I believe the mark is there now," and he turned toward his mother the other cheek, which he had kept carefully away from her up to this time. She saw the marks clearly and she trembled herself with sympathy and secret indignation.

"Well," she said, "and what did you do?"

"I remembered what I had promised you for this year, and took it—think of it, Mother—took it and never touched him! I just looked into his eyes, and said, 'If I should strike you back, I should lower myself to your level.' He laughed a great, scornful laugh, and said, 'You hear, boys? Morgan is turned preacher. You'd better wait, sir, before you lecture me on my behavior to the little ones, till you have pluck enough to defend them. I've heard about the last impudence I shall from a coward like you.' The boys laughed, and some of them said, 'Good for you, Osgood!' and I came home. I had done it for the sake of my promise to you! I'm stronger than he is any day; and you know, Mother, whether there's a drop of coward's blood in my veins. I thought you were the one to comfort me, though it isn't comfort I want so much, either. I just want you to release me from that promise, and let me go back and thrash him."

Mrs. Morgan's heart thrilled with silent thanksgiving. Her

boy's temper had been her greatest grief. His father was dead, and she had brought him up alone, and sometimes she was afraid her too-great tenderness had spoiled him. She had tried in vain to curb his passionate nature. It was a power which no bands could bind. She had concluded at last that the only hope was in enlisting his own powerful will, and making him resolve to conquer himself. Now, she realized, he had shown himself capable of self-control. In the midst of his anger he had remembered his pledge to her, and had kept it. He would yet be his own master—this brave boy of hers.

"Better heap coals of fire on his head?" she said quietly.

"Yes, he deserves a good scorching"—pretending to misunderstand her—"but I wouldn't have thought you'd be so revengeful."

"You know well enough what kind of coals I mean, and Who it

was that said, 'If thine enemy hunger, feed him; if he thirst, give him drink.' I cannot release you from your promise till the year for which you made it is over. I think the Master who told us to render good for evil, understood all the wants and passions of humanity better than any other teacher has ever understood them. I am sure that what He said must be wise and right and best. I want you to try His way first. If that fails, there will be time enough after this year to make a different experiment."

"Well, I promised you," he said, "and I'll show you that, at least, I'm strong enough to keep my word until you release me from it. I think, though, you don't quite know how hard it is."

Mrs. Morgan thought she *did* know how hard it is to a boy's nature to be called a coward, but she knew, also, that the truest bravery on earth is the bravery of endurance.

"Look out for the coals of fire!" she said smilingly, as her boy started off for school the next morning. "Keep a good watch, and I'm pretty sure you'll find them."

But he came home that night depressed and a little gloomy. There had always been a sort of rivalry between him and Dick Osgood, and now the boys seemed to have gone over to the stronger side, and he had that bitter feeling of humiliation and disgrace, which is as galling to a boy as the sense of defeat ever is to a man.

The weeks went on, and the feeling wore away a little. Still the memory of that blow rankled in Guy's mind, and made him unsocial and ill at ease. His mother watched him with some anxiety, but did not interfere. She had the true wisdom to leave him to learn some of the lessons of life alone.

At length came the last day of school, followed the next day by a picnic in which all the scholars were to join, superintended by their teachers. Guy Morgan hesitated a little, then decided to go.

The place selected was a lovely spot, known in all the neighborhood as "the old mill." It was on the banks of the Quassit River, where the stream ran fast, and the grass on its brink was green, and great trees with drooping boughs shut it away from the July sunlight.

Among the rest were Dick Osgood and his little sister Hetty, the one human being whom Dick seemed really and tenderly to love. The teacher's eyes were on him for this one day, thus he didn't venture to insult the older scholars or domineer over the little ones. He and Guy kept apart as much as they conveniently could, and Guy entered into the spirit of the day, and really enjoyed it more than he had enjoyed anything during the past two months.

Dinner was spread on the grass, and nothing partaken at home on black walnut tables, and from the best of dishes, was ever relished with half the zest which these picnickers evidenced as they devoured the food dished with pewter spoons out of crockery of every hue and kind.

They made dinner last as long as they could, and then they scattered here and there, some of them swinging in hammocks, and a group standing on the bridge, a few yards above the falls, and playing at fishing. Among the latter were Dick Osgood and his sister. Guy Morgan was a little distance away, with one of the teachers, pulling to pieces a curious flower and talking botany. Suddenly a wild cry rose above the falls. It was Dick Osgood's cry, "She's in, boys! Hetty's in the river, and I can't swim. Oh! Save her, save her! Will no one try?"

Before the words were out of his lips, they all saw Guy Morgan coming with flying feet—a race for life. He unbuttoned coat and vest as he ran, and cast them off as he neared the bridge. He kicked off his shoes, and threw himself over. They heard him strike the water. He went under, rose again, and then struck out toward the golden head, which rose just then for the second time. Everyone who stood there lived moments which seemed hours.

The boys with Mr. Sharp, the teacher with whom Guy had been talking, got a strong rope, and running down the stream, threw it on the water just above the falls, where Guy could reach it if he could get near the shore—*if*—

The water was very deep where Hetty had fallen in, and the river ran fast. It was sweeping the poor child on, and Dick Osgood convulsively clung to the bridge railing, sobbing and screaming. When she rose the third time, she was near the falls. A moment more and she would go over, down upon the jagged, cruel rocks below. But this time Guy Morgan caught her—caught her by her long, glistening golden hair. Mr. Sharp shouted to him. Guy saw the rope, and swam toward it, his strong right arm beating the water back with heavy strokes, his left motionless, holding his white burden.

"Oh God!" Mr. Sharp prayed fervently, "keep him up, spare his strength a little longer, a little longer!" A moment more and Guy lunged for the rope, clung to it desperately, and the boys and teacher gradually drew the line in over the slippery edge, out of the horrible, seething waters, and took them in their arms, both silent, motionless. Mr. Sharp spoke Guy's name, but he did not answer. Would either of them ever answer again?

Teachers and scholars alike went to work for their restoration. It was well that there was intelligent guidance, or their best efforts might have failed. Guy, being the stronger, was the first to revive.

"Is Hetty safe?" was his anxious question.

"Only God knows!" Mr. Sharp answered. "We're doing our best."

It was almost half an hour before Hetty opened her blue eyes. Meantime Dick had been utterly frantic and helpless. He had sobbed and groaned and prayed even, in a wild fashion of his own, which perhaps the pitying Father understood and answered. When he heard his sister's voice, he was like one beside himself with joy, until Mr. Sharp quieted him by a few low, firm words, which were audible to no one else.

Some of the older girls arranged one of the wagons, and getting into it, received Hetty into their arms.

Mr. Sharp drove home with Guy Morgan. When he reached his mother's gate, Guy insisted on going in alone. He thought it might alarm her to see someone helping him; besides, he wanted her a few minutes all by himself. So Mr. Sharp drove away, and Guy went in. His mother saw him coming and opened the door.

"Where have you been?" she cried, seeing his wet, disordered plight.

"In Quassit River, Mother, fishing out Hetty Osgood."

Then, while she was busying herself with preparations for his comfort, he quietly told his story. His mother's eyes were dim, and her heart throbbed chokingly.

"Oh, if you had been drowned, my boy, my darling!" she cried, hugging him close, wet as he was, as if she would hold him back from all danger forever. "If I had been there, Guy, I couldn't have let you do it."

"I went in after the coals of fire, Mother."

Mrs. Morgan knew how to laugh with her boy, as well as how to cry over him. "I've heard of people smart enough to set the river on fire," she half laughed/half cried, "but you are the first one I ever knew who went in there after the coals."

The next morning came a delegation of the boys, with Dick Osgood at their head. Everyone was there who had seen the blow which Dick struck, and heard his taunts afterward. They came into the sitting room, and had their say to Guy in front of his mother.

Dick was spokesman. "I have come," he said, "to ask you to forgive me. I struck you a mean, unjustifiable blow. You received it with noble contempt. To provoke you into fighting, I called you a coward, meaning to bring you down by some means to my own level. You bore that, too, with a greatness I was not great enough to understand. I do understand it now. I have seen you—all we boys have seen you—face to face with Death, and have seen that you were not afraid of him. You fought with him, and came off ahead; and we are all come to do honor to the bravest boy in town. And I, too, thank you for the life a great deal dearer and better worth saving than my own."

Dick broke down just there, for the tears choked him.

Guy was as grand in his forgiveness as he had been in his forbearance.

Hetty and her father and mother came afterward, and Guy found himself made a hero before he knew it. But none of it all moved him as did his mother's few fond words, and the pride in her joyful eyes. He had kept, with honor and with peace, his pledge to her, and he had his reward. He had not rejected the Master's way of peace.

ELEVEN

A PLACE IN THE SUN

Martha F. Simmonds

The ministry: Just a career and not a matter of conviction? So declared Jerry Wright, convinced his powerful father would get him the Mount Pleasant pulpit, the plum of all pastoral openings. Ben Craig sighed, being the son of "Tiny" Craig, a veteran of small, struggling churches. Was it right that men like his father should never be recognized, never honored?

And what chance then had the son against a Jerry Wright?

In the long, narrow attic of Hope Hall, a dozen young men were gathered at the west end, looking out the dormer windows. They sat around the same worn table that had witnessed heated sessions in their student days; but they could not realize that student days were over for them!

"I tell you, fellows," Jerry Wright said eagerly, "I am certain of a fine appointment. Dad has a lot of influence back home, and he knows the bishop personally. I'm trusting that I can cut some of this backwoods stuff. At any rate, I don't expect to be given a circuit. In fact, Dad's been angling some time for a pretty good thing for me."

Ben Craig looked out at the sun sinking behind the library tower. He knew what that appointment was! The Mount Pleasant Church, lovely, vine-covered, with a tolerant, encouraging congregation and a good salary—of course Jerry wanted it, and would likely get it, for Jerry's father was wealthy and powerful.

"How come you ever entered the ministry, Jerry?" James Brown asked curiously. "No, I really want to know. You are handsome and talented. Your father has money. And—if you'll forgive me—your zeal doesn't seem to run to religion."

Jerry laughed. "You guessed it, my zeal doesn't; but it runs to a good salary, and prestige. I haven't a bit of business brains—could no more take up Dad's work than I could be a milliner. And my talents aren't many, except a certain gift of speech, and that same attractive appearance you mentioned; hence—the ministry—where I figure both will count."

"You actually mean," said Mark Chesney, "that you're in it just for—money?"

"Money—and prestige—my place in the sun, if you will!"

"*Well!* I've often suspected it, but I never expected to hear you admit it!"

"Why not?" Jerry stretched languidly back in his chair. "Does a farmer till the soil because he's passionately in love with it? Does a banker begin business out of a desire to save money for the world? Other men go into vocations for motives of self-advancement. Why shouldn't a minister? This divine calling stuff is the bunk, and you all know it!"

"I don't think it is," James maintained stoutly. "That is, I think the ministry's different. Other things are just serving self or other men, but the ministry is serving God."

"And who is God?"

Mark's face was a study. "Jerry Wright, if the bishop, if any

of the professors here heard you say that, you'd not get a charge this fall!"

Jerry laughed easily. "But they'll *not* hear it, my boy! Here we are, twelve of us who have gone through the seminary together, the inner circle of the graduating class, keeping our commencement pact to meet here at this time. I can speak my mind here."

"But you shouldn't be allowed to preach, with such an attitude."

"Do you have any idea how many ministers have that attitude?" Jerry leaned forward.

Ben Craig rose suddenly to his feet. "Jerry," he said, "it's unfair of you to do this when we're about to separate, to take up what is, for most of us at least, a real lifework. I don't feel like your farmer or your banker. My heart's in this thing, and whether I preach in a brownstone church or on a circuit, I'll preach with all there is of me!"

"It'll be the circuit, no doubt, Little Bennie," Jerry smiled. "You're too quiet. You ought to assert yourself. You'll never get anywhere. Why—you've been four years on the campus and no one really knows you."

"How dare you, Jerry!" Mark hotly defended. "There's not a one of us whom Little Bennie hasn't helped. There's—"

"Sure, but do you know him? You couldn't even name his hometown or tell how many are in his family."

"Well—" lamely. "But he lives two stalls away, and—"

"I'll answer that, Mark," said Little Bennie quietly. "Jerry and I come from the same conference. My town is a little one of about fifteen hundred people, and my father is minister there. He went here for his training, because his folks lived in this state then. There are just three of us. If I've been quiet here, it's because I was sort of brought up in that tradition, to keep still about things, that's all. It's Father's way. I'm short like he is—they called him Tiny Craig in school, and I expect I'll follow pretty much in his footsteps."

"You say—Tiny Craig? Seems to me that my father said something—he used to go here, too, you know—" James looked at Ben doubtfully.

"I hardly think so. Father's not one to make a splash."

After the circle reluctantly broke up, Mark Chesney threw a restraining arm around Ben's shoulders.

"I say, Little Bennie, that was pretty raw of Jerry. Don't mind. And I don't think he'll have a better charge than you. Not if the board knows what it's doing. He's thin-skinned and hollow, and you're just solid gold."

"I am to you—but you know me. Jerry'll get the Mount Pleasant Church all right, and I don't begrudge him. And I expect I'll get the circuit. But I can hardly stand it to see someone like that walk into the easy places."

"I know. You deserve so much more, old man."

"It isn't of myself I'm thinking!" Ben protested impatiently. "It's my father."

Mark stood, waiting. After all this time, was Bennie going to finally speak?

"My father's the finest man in the world, Mark," he said, his clear gray eyes looking up into the troubled blue ones. "You must understand that. But we've always been on small charges, gone to run-down places. Soon as Father gets the church built up, he is moved on and someone else reaps the profits. Father never speaks up for himself. Jerry would call him a failure. I've never gone to conference with him, for I didn't want to see him stand on the sidelines while people like Jerry, who exploit the ministry for their own gain, get ahead. It hurts me more than you can know to think of going there and seeing what I know I will."

"Little Bennie," Mark's eyes filled, "you make me want to break down like a schoolgirl. I know just what your father's like, the same fine person you are."

"Durable, but not flashy," Ben smiled painfully, "and the flashy ones seem to get the plums. I'm not greedy for myself, but I'd like just one plum for Father."

Mark was silent a little while. "Well, Little Bennie, I happen to be entering the ministry for the same reason you are. My heart's in it. I can't do anything else; but I'll think, and I'll pray. And I believe in prayer. You leave tonight, don't you? Are you and Jerry going together?"

"Hadn't you heard? His father's been to New York on a business trip. Jerry's to get into his Pullman tonight. I'm riding day coach. Father expressly told me to take a Pullman, but I've saved a lot in ways like that, without telling him. It was enough that he insisted I come all the way here for the reunion. So Jerry and I will be going together—and yet apart."

"Wish I could go with you."

"I do, too, old man! Funny thing is, we're both going early. Father says his old crowd is to have a banquet before the meeting begins. But Jerry's going to the bishop's banquet! At least, the bishop will be there, and Jerry and his father are invited. The bishop's from his hometown, you know."

"Don't let it get you down, Little Bennie!" Mark was encouraging.

"I won't,

"Think

"Mark, i̶ ̶ ̶ ̶ ̶ ̶ ̶ ̶ ̶ ̶xt I'd choose. It would be 'The heart knoweth its own bitterness.

"Oh, Ben! I know your father wouldn't react that way!"

"No, of course. If he knew this he'd choose a text like, 'Yet have I not seen the righteous forsaken, nor his seed begging bread.'"

In the train, Ben Craig thought and thought over the situation until it seemed to him he had never drunk so deeply of bitterness and despair. The world seemed all wrong, and a sense of injustice rankled within him. His personal pride in his father, he felt, was about to be struck a savage blow through the preeminence of the Wright father and son.

When the train pulled in, he looked out. As he had expected, he saw his father's stooped shoulders and slender form, the eager face, so worn and tired.

"Let's get away quickly, my boy, before the crowd catches us." What matter the crowd to them? Father must not dream of what he felt. He asked and answered questions, assuming a tone of well-being and gaiety which he did not feel. "I just saw Clark Evans. He asked particularly after you."

"Yes. Marian wrote me and asked me to come over for a few days, if I could, after the meeting."

"You must go, Son."

"I'll see how it turns out. I may have to go directly to my charge." He knew his father suspected that he had dreams of Marian as mistress of a parsonage. His father could not know that he was waiting to ask her; waiting to see just how small a circuit charge the Reverend Craig's son would receive, after all the Jerry Wrights were satisfied.

"I guess you can have a few days if you want them."

"I'm just a young cub at this game, Father; can't hope for favors like you old tried-and-true warriors." Later that evening, Ben remembered those words and the pleased response on his father's face—remembered them so gladly.

The Craigs were a little late at the banquet. Ben didn't mind. He rather dreaded seeing the other patient, tired ministers that his father's crowd would be.

"But, Father—is it here?" They entered a large hotel.

"Surely, Son. I told you it was a banquet."

They shot upstairs in the elevator, checked their belongings, and opened the door of a small private dining room. Within were some twenty-five men seated at a table. As they entered, one rose from the opposite end.

"The late Reverend Craig and son!" he said, dramatically. From the nearest end, one turned instantly. "Here are your chairs, waiting." Mr. Craig took Ben by the arm and piloted him proudly to that distinguished figure. "Bishop Warren, this is my son, Ben."

The bishop took Ben's hand and put an arm around his shoulders. "A great son of a great father, I can see that," he said kindly. "I ask nothing better than that you follow in your father's footsteps."

When Ben turned again to his father, he found him surrounded by men, joking, saying the intimate friendly things that belong to the words one has for someone respected, admired— even loved. His father was watching and drew him into the circle, introducing him. Ben recognized the big names of the conference, the proud names. Far down near the end of the table sat Jerry Wright, beside his father. The two boys nodded at each other.

Ben Craig never knew, afterward, what he had eaten. It might have been sawdust for all his realization of it. He had not yet recovered from the wonder of his father's presence in this company, when the bishop rose, and tapped on his glass for silence. After a very brief welcome, he said:

"And now, gentlemen, I come to the event of the evening. On my right is a man you all know and love—to some of you he was Tiny Craig in school, to some of you he is just plain John. Most of you were my classmates, some of you were his. But he has come to be included in these banquets, just for his own sake.

"You know what he is, but I think I'd like to tell you in his presence, a few of the things he means to his bishop. I have plenty of 'flashes' in this conference, plenty of brilliant flashing folk to fill the big pulpits; but John Craig, to me, has meant a solid rock of dependability. He's the one minister I have whom I can send into a run-down charge and know it will be built up. I can send him into a bickering community and know he will patch up the quarrels. He can make a success out of an impossible situation. And because he serves God and not man, he will move on and let another take the reward. Many of you have followed him. You know what I mean.

"I have offered John Craig the best in the conference. He has turned it down, because he believes his talent lies in the places where the church seems about to fail.

"John," he turned to the little minister at his side, "you are here at my right because I delight to honor you, as I always do. And your friends in this little group want you to know that they delight to honor you too. You have just concluded your twenty-fifth year in this conference. Didn't think we remembered, did you? But we did. And we have some little gifts. Here's a watch that will keep perfect time for you to catch the train to the next desert you'll make blossom like the rose. And here's a Bible from which to preach those good sermons, with our names and our pictures in it, and your name on it. Gentlemen, I present to you John Craig, by far the finest soul I have ever known, and the most valuable minister in the conference! He will never let me do him honor in public, but I repeat it to you, and you will bear me out—*he is the most valuable minister in the conference.*"

Ben Craig's heart was pounding in his very ears. Oh, tonight was incredible! His father stood, and when the applause had finally died down, he said very quietly, "Brothers in the faith—" and Ben felt at home.

Afterward, the bishop said, "And we must have a word from John Craig's son. He's here with us tonight, one of us. Will you speak a word, Ben?"

"My father's friends," Ben said, "I am proud to be here tonight. For only I can tell you how great a man my father is. You see, he is so real, so sincere, that I never knew he was the bishop's friend. But I've been proud of him all my life, and all my life I've listened to such things as he said tonight. I'm glad to be one of you, and I know I will succeed…because he is my father."

The most wonderful event of all was yet to happen! After the banquet was over, and Jerry Wright and his father had come up to meet the Reverend Craig, the bishop drew Ben aside.

"My boy," he said, "how would you like to go to Mount Pleasant? I'm sending you there for your father's sake, and for your own. I believe in you—and one sacrifice in the family is enough. This reward he would never accept, but he will get it through you. I'm giving you the best start in my power, and I know you'll make something of it. Tell him, he'll be happy."

Before he slept that night, Ben wrote to Marian to tell her the good news and to ask her to be ready to answer a certain question when he came to see her very soon. Just as his eyes were closing, he remembered, "The heart knoweth its own bitterness," and smiled in the darkness to think of his vast ignorance so little a while ago. "Yet have I not seen the righteous forsaken," he exulted, "nor his seed begging bread!"

MARTHA F. SIMMONDS *wrote some of the most memorable stories to come out of the first half of the twentieth century.*

TWELVE

A GIRL AGAINST
A BLIZZARD

Helen Rezatto

Not all heroes are bedecked with medals and lauded by the media. And many a hero lives and dies without even realizing the value of that inner strength and courage that we label heroic.

It seemed an odd day for heroics anyhow. A spring thaw? So it seemed…but then, off in the distance, an ominous blackness against the bright spring sky.

The morning of March 15 was pleasant and sunny as William Miner, a farmer near Center, North Dakota, completed his chores. A thaw had set in, and the snow in the fields was patchy.

"Snow should be gone by night," he reported optimistically to his wife when he came in at noon. But after the couple had eaten a leisurely meal, Miner glanced out the kitchen window. "Oh, no!" he exclaimed. In the northwest a black, billowy cloud loomed over the horizon. It moved stealthily, inexorably, its dark bluish edges spreading across the sky toward the unsuspecting sun.

Blanche Miller spoke with the sure instinct of a homesteader. "Spring norther!"

They watched the advance of the formless, faceless monster. Abruptly, Miner said, "You get the stock in. I'm going to school to get the kids. I don't like the looks of it."

Miner piled on his storm clothes, saddled Kit, his best horse, and started down the slushy road to the school two and a half miles away. By now the apparition had writhed and swelled its way to overpower the sun. All nature was poised, breathless, apprehensive. Then an avalanche of blinding snow and wind slammed into the horse and rider. Miner fought through it to the school barn, tied Kit among the other stomping, nervous horses, and hurried into the schoolhouse.

The teacher and pupils had observed the approach of the blizzard, but were still pretending to concentrate on lessons. Although many children had their own horses and sleighs in the school barn, the established blizzard rule was that no child should leave unless called for by a parent.

"Hi, Dad!" fifteen-year-old Hazel Miner exclaimed. She turned to her brother, Emmet, eleven, and her sister, Myrdith, eight. "I guess somebody doesn't trust us to drive old Maude home!"

Her father smiled briefly. "Hurry! Get your wraps—here are extra scarves."

Hazel bent down to fasten her sister's overshoes and said to Emmet, "Don't forget your history book." *Hazel is wonderfully dependable,* Miner thought. *She always far surpasses expectations.*

He carried Myrdith outside to their homemade sleigh with its rounded canvas cover, settled the two children in the straw lining the bottom, covered them with two blankets and an old fur robe. Then Hazel perched on the driver's seat while her father hitched

Maude to the sleigh. Above the belligerent wind he shouted to Hazel, "Stay right here! I'll get Kit and lead the way."

Maude was facing the north gate toward home. She had always been placid and easily managed, but now a thunderclap startled her, and she bolted, swerving through the south gate. Hazel, knocked off balance and hardly able to see through the swirling snow, did not realize at first that Maude was headed in the wrong direction. She shouted to the wide-eyed younger children, "Don't worry, we'll beat Dad and Kit home! Maude knows the way."

Hazel could do nothing to control the horse, for the reins trailed out of reach beneath the tugs. Finally, Maude slowed to a walk and stopped, her sides heaving.

Emmet called, "Are we home? Did we beat Dad?"

Hazel stepped down into the snow. Through the dizzying gloom she could not tell whether they were on a road or in a field.

The whole world had become a white-foaming, lashing sea, threatening to swallow them all. Panting for breath, she crawled back into the driver's seat with the reins. "No, we're not home yet, but I think we're close. Now that Maude's calmed down, she'll know the way."

Maude, repentant about her escapade, plowed along through the growing gloom. Once she plunged into a low place filled with water from the spring thaws and choked with ice and new snow. A tug came unhitched and Hazel, stepping down into the chilling slush, reached her bare hands into the water, fumbling for the tug, and fastened it. By the time she led Maude out of the water, she was soaked to the waist and her clothes were turning into heavy armor. Then, close by, she saw the top of a fence post sticking above the snow. They dug into the snow until she located the barbed wire. The fence would lead them to a farm and safety.

Emmet got out to see what she was doing. Together, they broke off the crystal mask that had formed over Maude's face. They grasped Maude's bridle to keep her on the fence line, but a huge drift blocked the way and they had to turn off the course. Frantically trying to get back, Emmet and Hazel pawed for the wire or another post to guide them. They could find neither. (The gate, buried in the big drift, opened to a farm only two hundred feet away.)

Almost suffocated from the onslaught of wind and snow, the two climbed back into the sleigh. Stubbornly, Maude kept on until the sleigh lurched over a concealed obstacle. It tipped over on its side, and the children were thrown against the canvas top.

Again Hazel and Emmet got out. Blindly, they pushed, they heaved, they pulled. But the sleigh, jammed into the snow, was too heavy for them to lift.

In the howling darkness, Hazel realized that it was up to her, the oldest. She fumbled into the canvas. "See," she said, "we're in a little cave. We'll fix it nice and cozy."

Since the sleigh was on its side, the narrow wooden floor formed a low wall to the east and the canvas top (uncurtained at the ends) made a tunnel-like tent. In the dark, Hazel found the blankets and robe. Despite her now-crippled hands, she placed the two blankets on the canvas "floor." Following her instructions, Emmet and Myrdith lay down, curled together tightly. The wind snarled through the north opening, and Hazel tried to improvise a curtain with the fur robe. It blew down again and again. Finally she tucked the robe around her brother and sister.

The hellish wind tore and ripped at the canvas top. Hazel snatched at the flapping scraps and piled over the robe all she could salvage. There was only one way to keep them in place—to fling herself on top of them. Now there was nothing between the three children and the blizzard except some dangling strips blowing from the bare wooden framework.

The snow fell incessantly. Three human specks lay motionless, their minds and bodies stupefied, benumbed by the terrifying, pulsating forces. Hazel roused herself. "Emmet! Myrdith!" she shouted. "You mustn't close your eyes. Punch each other! I'll count to a hundred. Make your legs go up and down as though you're running. Begin—one, two, three—" She could feel the small legs moving underneath her. She tried to move her own; her brain instructed her legs, but she wasn't sure what they did.

"I'm tired. Can't we stop?" begged Myrdith's muffled voice.

"No!" came the stern answer. "We're only at seventy-one."

Next Hazel ordered, "Open and close your fingers one hundred times inside your mittens."

Emmet stuck his head out from under the robe. "Come on, Hazel, get under here. We'll make room."

"No, I can't." Little warmth her ice-mantled clothes would provide the others! "Everything blows away. I've got to hold it down. Besides, I'm not very cold. Let's sing 'America, the Beautiful,' like we did in our opening exercises this morning."

From underneath the robe came the thin, childish voices and the words they had sung only that morning—but a hundred years away. *For purple mountain majesties above the fruited plain.* They sang all four verses.

"Let's pray to God to help us," suggested Myrdith. "Now I lay me down to sleep—" she began.

Hazel interrupted, "No, not that one. Let's say 'Our Father' instead." Solemnly they chanted the prayer.

On into the endless night Hazel directed them—in exercises, stories, songs, prayers; several times she sat up in the never-ending snow and forced her nearly paralyzed fingers to break the crusts that formed around Myrdith's and Emmet's legs; then she brushed and scraped away the creeping menace.

She said to the two children over and over, "Remember, you mustn't go to sleep—even if I do. Promise me you won't, no matter how sleepy you get. Keep each other awake! Promise?"

They promised.

More than once Myrdith voiced the question: "Why doesn't Daddy find us?"

———

When William Miner discovered his children had disappeared from the schoolyard, he urged Kit mercilessly through the fast-forming drifts, sure that Maude had gone home. His wife met him at the door. They gazed, horror-stricken, into each other's eyes.

Immediately, he gave the alarm over the rural party lines. Nearly forty men, risking their lives, were soon moving slowly, persistently, over the fields and roads between Miner's farm and the school. They paused at farms to change teams, to treat frostbite, to gulp coffee, to devise new plans. All the other children were safe in their homes. The men found nothing.

The wind became a sixty-mile-an-hour gale, the temperature dropped to zero, the gray became utter blackness. And the maddening snow kept falling. The searchers had to give up until daylight.

Next morning one group of searchers reported tracks made by a small sleigh and a horse which went out the south schoolhouse gate—then were obliterated by the falling snow. Quickly, the search was reorganized. Men with teams and sleighs, men on horseback, men on foot fanned out for half a mile. Back and forth they forced their way across the shrouded land.

At two o'clock on Tuesday afternoon, twenty-five hours from the time the Miner children had disappeared, searchers spotted something in a pasture two miles south of the school. It was an overturned sleigh. Next to it, like a sentry, a ghostlike horse stood motionless but still alive. They saw the bulky snow-covered mound under the arch of the naked, skeleton-like staves.

The rigid body of a girl lay face down with her unbuttoned coat flung wide. Her arms were stretched over her brother and sister, sheltering and embracing them in death as she had in life.

Tenderly, the men lifted her, then slowly removed the matted robe and torn canvas pieces that she had been holding down with her body. Underneath were Myrdith and Emmet, dazed and partially frozen but alive. They had promised never to fall into the dread sleep from which Hazel knew they could never waken.

Today, on the courthouse grounds in the town of Center, these words are engraved on a granite monument rising, like a challenge, above the plains:

In
Memory
of
HAZEL MINER
April 11, 1904
March 16, 1920

To the dead a tribute
To the living a memory
To posterity an inspiration

THE STORY OF HER LIFE AND OF HER
TRAGIC DEATH IS RECORDED IN THE
ARCHIVES OF OLIVER COUNTY.

STRANGER, READ IT.

HELEN REZATTO *wrote for popular magazines during the second half of the twentieth century.*

THIRTEEN

THE RADIO
NOTWITHSTANDING

G. E. Wallace

Who should Mr. Tower send to the doomed town: James Gordon or Wes Weaver? Weaver was a veteran flyer, true; but Tower decided to send Gordon—for one very important reason.

———

James Gordon rode the storm until it split in two and began to fight with itself. Then he bailed out. He had ridden it from the airport until he had sent his plane far into the jumble of hills and the upthrust peaks beyond Granite Ridge. Then the winds began to battle each other, wild swirling currents leaping up from the ravines, tearing and thrusting at the wild gale that was racing above the peaks. A strut had snapped—a wing had given way—and James Gordon was in the air, hoping that when he did land, he would not be dragged far. Then he turned his attention to the matter at hand. Where was Pinegrove? For James Gordon was like that.

———

The head of the Northern Aviation Company, Tower by name, frowned. Rains, heavy rains, had swollen the mountain streams, so the radio report said. And a message had come through from Pinegrove asking for help. Pinegrove, situated amid the jumbled hills of the northern section of the state, was cut off, sickness had broken out, an epidemic was threatening. "Send antitoxin!" they had radioed imperatively.

Mr. Tower stroked his chin. He looked out of the window of his little office and studied the sky. Even before he called for the weather forecasts, he knew what they would be. In the west, visibility, zero. High winds in the mountains. Snow or cold rain falling.

"Whom," a ground mechanic in the office at the time asked, "are you going to send?"

Mr. Tower considered. "I think," he finally said, "I'll send Jimmy, if Jimmy will go."

"Jimmy!" the ground mechanic exclaimed. Not that Jimmy wasn't good. He was. But there were others; Wes Weaver for example. Wes was a veteran flyer. "I'd think you'd pick Wes," he suggested.

Mr. Tower considered again. "Wes is good," he agreed, "better than Jimmy in some respects—but..."

The ground mechanic waited in patient silence.

"But," the manager lifted the receiver of the phone on his desk, "but Jimmy has a peculiar, a very peculiar, mind. Ever notice that? He gets an idea, one idea, firmly fixed, and no other idea has a chance."

The ground mechanic nodded. "I understand," he said. Success—failure. Jim could think of one, but not of both. Now if Wes went, Wes would be thinking of getting there, but thinking, too, of his chances of getting out if the going got bad. Jim, on the other hand, would be thinking of only one thing.

"You want me to get to Pinegrove with this antitoxin," James Gordon said, standing, a few minutes later, before Mr. Tower, head of the Northern Aviation Company.

A nod. "The town's cut off. The railroad's blocked by a slide. The bridges are out on the highway. And there's sickness."

"I'll do my best," James said and made ready to turn.

"You've got it? You're to get there! Understand?"

A nod. "Pinegrove's over past Granite Ridge, about one hundred and fifty miles north, isn't it?" Jimmy asked.

"Right. There's Meadowdale, then Summitville, and then Pinegrove."

Not that it would do much good to name those towns. The chances were that Jim would pass them without seeing them. For the scudding clouds were racing low, trailing gray fingers of mist, clutching at the treetops.

"I wish you luck!" Mr. Tower said.

And in the teeth of a gale Jimmy left.

The first hundred miles was easy. You rode high above the flat, level country—you kept the plane headed north—and you didn't have to worry. Granite Ridge was ahead, and you'd know when you came to Granite Ridge. The mountain would send up an air current that would buffet the plane. You could tell when you got over Granite Ridge all right!

Jim kept his eyes on his instrument board, and looked at all times at the precious bundle of antitoxin. Well-wrapped it was, with a parachute attached.

"If you can't land, drop it!" the chief had ordered.

Jim had nodded.

"Attract their attention; then drop it!"

"I'll do my best," Jimmy had said. If he couldn't land? But he was rather good at landing a plane. He'd try to get down.

And then suddenly the plane tried to turn over backward.

Jim smiled. Granite Ridge was below.

He fought the wind. He whistled softly to himself as he drove into the fury of the gale in the hills. But he rode high, and the miles were clicked off.

Five minutes—ten. Jim calculated. He wished he knew just where he was. He wished—and then luck was with him. The storm clouds opened for one-half second. A long finger of light shot down from the upper sunlit heights, the finger picked out a huddle of buildings, and Jimmy knew he was on his course.

Of course the town might be either Meadowdale or Summitville. But he was on his course, and he'd risk dropping down for a look later.

And then ice began to form. Jimmy frowned. That was bad. But the plane was handling all right—so far. He debated as to what he'd better do. Then shrugged. As long as she responded fairly well, he'd take a chance. You couldn't do much about ice anyway, except hope you had luck.

You couldn't do much about a gale either, especially when the gale divided into separate parts and the air currents began to fight among themselves. A rising torrent would twist one wing while the other would be wrenched by a current that was going in the opposite direction.

Jimmy continued—and then he seized the antitoxin and bailed out. For when your plane goes to pieces under you, there's nothing else left to do.

Through the gray veil of the storm clouds he fell. He counted slowly. There was no use giving way to a blind panic of fear. If he ripped the cord too soon, he might tangle in the falling plane. If too late—Jimmy shrugged. *I wish,* he thought while falling, *I knew whether that town I passed was Meadowdale or Summitville! At any rate Pinegrove is to the north.*

A tree nearly speared him. A boulder did strike him on the back of his head. Jimmy lay still. And the world went round—and round—and round.

Then Jimmy was on his feet, trying to walk. And his face was pointed north.

I've got to get there! he said to himself.

He felt better after he'd gone a half-mile or so. His head had cleared, the ache had turned from a splitting pain to a dull throb. *Lucky for me,* he thought, *it wasn't a snapped leg! If it had been, I'd never get there with the antitoxin!*

The wind increased as he climbed higher and higher up the slope of the mountain. He wished he knew where the pass across the range was. It must be somewhere. He could hunt for it, of course, but if he did, *I might get lost,* he thought. For one thing, he knew Pinegrove was north, due north, straight ahead.

The trees gave way to gnarled little caricatures. The caricatures gave way to mere shrubs. Then rocks, ice-glazed rocks.

I can't walk, Jim thought. *I can't*—he tried to catch his breath—*I can't walk against this gale!*

He crawled. *The summit must be—ahead!*

Once a deep cleft stopped his advance. He shrugged. Carefully he turned—at right angles—and crept along. The cold was intense. *It must be ten, maybe twenty below!* The wind was *bitterly* cold. It cut and chilled him to the very marrow. And he slipped, too, on the ice-glazed rocks. His hands and knees were cut and rasped and raw.

Jim crept on.

And suddenly he was heading north again. The cleft ended.

He found it easier going on the other side of the summit. Rocks—then shrubs—then trees.

Jim stood in the lee of one tree and regained his breath. It was warmer down here. He wished he knew if that town, behind, had been Meadowdale or Summitville. He *wished* he knew!

And while Jim rested, the radio waves were carrying a message to the listening world. "Storm increasing—gale increasing—driving rain on lower slopes swelling the streams that were going down."

Jim walked on. Then stopped.

Before him was a river—in flood. He stared at its dark, fast-flowing water. Swim? He might, and yet the current was swift, almost too swift.

A tree floated down the stream, followed by a mat of willows that had been torn from the muddy banks.

Jim stood watching. Down the stream the tree floated to yonder point where the bank jutted out, and then the slanting current caught it and took it across, almost to the far bank!

And the willow mat also swirled across, almost to that far side!

Jim acted. He broke sapling poles. He tugged and lifted, dragging out alders and willows from the soft ooze of the bank. And he bore them down the bank to where that point of land jutted out.

Then he wove them, as well as he could, until he had a semi-solid raft. He bound the whole together with lengths of wild grapevines torn from the branches of the trees.

And then he was on the river, and his sapling mat was swirling, turning, spinning, this way and that, but heading across the stream.

He had to jump from it and wade. But he was over!

"A last report from a doomed town," the radio was sending another message out, "from a town cut off from help!"

James Gordon staggered down a deserted street. James Gordon wondered about that. He did not know that fear, and the orders of the doctors, had established a home quarantine.

I wonder, he thought, *what town this is.* If only he knew whether that other town had been Meadowdale or Summitville! But he didn't.

He paused at one building, where a light was burning.

He entered.

"Buddy," he said to a young fellow who sat before what he did not recognize, but what was a transmitter, "could you tell me if this town's Pinegrove?"

The operator was busy. The operator frowned. Static was giving him a lot of trouble. And besides—

"Just a minute," he said, scowling. He had not caught the question clearly. "I'm busy! I'm telling the world that this is the doomed town that no one can reach!"

G. E. WALLACE *wrote during the first half of the twentieth century. All of his inimitable stories deal with that intangible line between success and failure, in terms of both career and lifestyle.*

FOURTEEN

THE WAY OF THE CROSS

Margaret E. Sangster Jr.

Vera was deeply troubled. True, her work for the overworked pastor of the rather shabby church was needed—but she was so tired of being poor! And now here came this wonderful offer, at more than twice the salary. Why not take it?

———

Vera Franklin typed the next Sunday's sermon with trouble in her heart. The trouble was so acute that she was all but unconscious of the beautiful words that she was typing.

I really should take it, she told herself. *If I stay here, it'll be the same work year after year, and I'll die poor! I can't ever hope to get a raise in salary; they're paying the utmost limit already. I'm a good stenographer, too, and I deserve a chance.* With one nervous finger she banged out a final period and paused to contemplate her work.

Yes, Vera realized it again as she surveyed the rows of neat, accurate typing, she was a good stenographer. She was far too good to be wasted in the dingy parish house of a poverty-swept, although, busy church. Of course her work in the parish house was interesting. She copied sermons, such as the one which she was now typing, sent out bulletins, arranged club meetings, took minutes, and visited throughout the parish.

"I don't know how I'd ever manage without you, Miss Franklin," the pastor, Reverend Williams, had said hundreds of times; "you run the church and the congregations and me," he laughed gently, "in such a wonderful way. I don't know what we'd do if you left us. I only wish that I could pay you all that the job is worth."

Vera had looked at the pastor. Looking, she saw a man verging onto middle age, with kind tired eyes and a glowing smile. She had smiled, in answer, and had said, "You pay me quite enough. Don't you worry."

She had meant it, then, too. Temptation, in the shape of Commercial Products, Incorporated, had not yet come to her.

Perhaps it was fate that made Richard Terry wander into the parish house one noontime when the girls' club was having a fifteen-minute meeting and a basket lunch. The church stood just a stone's throw from the factory which controlled, and was controlled by, Commercial Products, Incorporated. Richard Terry, general manager of the factory, although he was but shortly out of college, had already attained a large and important position there. Unkind people said that he had gone far because his grandfather was the founder of the business; honest folk said that his success was due to his ability, his unfailing instinct, and his cleverness.

Nothing more than an adventurous sense of curiosity, however, had drawn him into the parish house that particular noon. He had heard the sound of laughter and music as he was passing by, and he had wanted to see what caused it. Embarrassment held him rooted to the spot when he discovered that he had stepped into a room which was teeming with chattering, sandwich-munching girls.

Vera Franklin had been busy with the girls, making them com-

fortable, arranging chairs, performing cordial introductions. She glanced up when a sudden hush fell over the room and saw the flushed young man in the doorway. Calmly, pleasantly, instantly she left her charges and hurried forward to meet him. "Suppose," she said with a smile, "you come into the study and I'll see if there's anything that I can do—"

She left the sentence unfinished as she led Richard Terry past the doorway and into the pastor's study. When the safety of that study had been gained, Richard spoke. "Whew!" he exclaimed. "I never saw so many girls all at once in my whole life."

Vera smiled. "They meet here twice a week," she explained. "It's one of our social clubs. But now," she paused, "is there anything that I can tell you, or any way in which I can help you? I'm the parish house secretary."

Richard Terry tried to explain. "I heard music as I was passing," he said, "and it awakened my curiosity. So I came in and I very nearly lived to regret it; but you can tell me one thing, now that I'm here. Have you ever considered another job? Any girl who can handle a crowd the way you do is too efficient to be wasted in church work. You see, I need a secretary. I'm Richard Terry, and I'm manager of Commercial Products, Incorporated. Our factory is across the street from you."

Vera nodded. "I know your factory," she said. "Incidentally, many of the girls who terrified you happen to be your own employees."

Richard laughed. "You see," he exclaimed, "it's just as I said! I need somebody who can manage my employees and point them out to me! Won't you come to my office and talk it over, Miss—" he hesitated until Vera supplied the name, "Miss Franklin? Talk business, I mean."

Vera hesitated briefly before she made an answer. "Why," she said at last, "I've always been quite satisfied here, Mr. Terry. I've never thought of changing."

Richard looked thoughtfully around the shabby parish house study. His gaze took in its every threadbare spot. "Without knowing what they pay you," he said, "I think I can safely promise to double your salary!"

That was the beginning of it all. Of course Vera called at Richard Terry's office. *Not that I want the job,* she reasoned with herself; *but I might as well see whether or not I could rate a position outside the church, in a real business organization.* She went over to the factory in a spirit of mental defiance, defiance not against the church or against herself, but against some intangible thing. *I belong in church work,* she argued, as she went; *it suits me and I like it, but still,* a little idea nagged at her brain, *I'd be interested to know if that man actually meant it when he said he'd pay me twice as much as I'm making now.*

Richard Terry's office was quite magnificent when seen after the parish house study. Vera, as she was shown into the room, was struck by the elegance of the deep leather chairs and the luxury of the walnut wall paneling. Her eyes went longingly toward the latest model typewriter that stood in the corner. She had used the old typewriter at the church for so long that it fairly wheezed with age. *I could do exquisite work on a machine like that,* she told herself, as she answered Richard Terry's cordial greeting.

A moment later she was sitting in a chair beside his desk and chatting away with him as though she had known him all her life.

"You must think I'm crazy," the young manager of Commercial Products, Incorporated, told her frankly, "offering to hire a girl whose work I know nothing about. But I could see at a glance that you've a genius for management, and the sort of tact that is a priceless gift in a private secretary. The way you got me out of that crowded room," he chuckled, "was a masterpiece of diplomacy."

Vera joined in his mirth. "Weren't the girls excited, too, when I came back!" she told him. "But I think it's only fair to explain to you that I've decided that I don't want to make a change. I'm very happy over at the church; the minister's a darling and he depends on me in every way. It isn't that I think I'm indispensable—no one is. But I do feel that the church can't pay much money for help, and that anyone else, who is willing to take on the job at my salary, would be inefficient. I wonder if you understand what I mean?"

Richard Terry smiled into Vera's earnest face. "Yes, I understand exactly what you mean," he said. "It makes me want to have you work for me more than ever. One can buy efficiency, but loyalty is a rare gift. I'd be prepared to start you at—" he named a figure that quite took away Vera's breath. "Suppose I give you a sample letter now so that we can see how the dictation goes?"

Vera had risen to her feet, however, and was nervously clasping and unclasping her slender hands. "I'd rather not take the sample letter," she said. Desperately she tried to express herself, "Oh, I feel like saying, 'Get thee behind me, Satan!' I shouldn't leave the church and I know it. Yet, when I think of all the things that I could buy and all the things I could do and all the money that I could save, well, you're making it very hard! I'm going to run back to my work now."

Richard Terry looked keenly at Vera's flushed face. "If you were any other girl," he said, "I'd think you were being clever and stalling along; that you were trying to get me interested to the point of offering you more money. But somehow I don't think that you're being clever; I merely think you're being honest. Understand my point of view, Miss Franklin, when I tell you that I won't promise not to bother you any more. When I see something that I want, and I don't mean private secretaries alone, I go after that something!"

With flushed cheeks Vera left Richard Terry's office. She walked back to the church with tumult in her heart. She went straight into the pastor's study and began to type the next Sunday's sermon, and even the beautiful words of it left her quiet and without any sensation of thrill. *I'm an idiot,* she told herself as she typed. *I should take that job. I really, really should.*

During the weeks that followed her interview in Richard Terry's office, Vera saw the young man frequently. The meetings were casual ones which happened when she was hurrying out of the parish house to do an errand, when she was coming in of a morning, or when she was leaving in the evening. Once or twice he walked beside her to the subway and they chatted of this and that. Always, in some way, he managed to insinuate a word about the job that was waiting for her if she wanted to accept it.

"I don't want to take it," Vera answered him every time. "I'm going to stay where I am. Church work suits me better than the other sort."

One day, then, she saw the coat. It was a beautiful fur coat that had been reduced after a hard winter in which sales had been few. It was luxury personified, the kind of a coat of which no sensible parish house secretary would dare dream. Yet Vera, looking at it, realized suddenly that she could do more than dream about it. She could possess it if she earned the salary which Commercial Products, Incorporated, had offered her.

The upshot of the matter was that she went into the store and tried on the coat. When she found that it fitted her and that it was most becoming, she knew that her resolutions were slipping. "I can't take it now," she said to the saleswoman who had helped her try on the coat. "But I'll think about it," she added weakly.

While on her way to work she had seen the coat. She came into the parish house and hung up her outer garments with a feeling of intense martyrdom and misery. The same old grind lay ahead of her—the girls' club, the boys' club, the mothers' meeting, the visits to querulous sick people, the midweek address to be neatly typed, and the minutes for the trustees' meeting to be put in order.

She settled down to the shabby wheezing typewriter and began to put the minutes in order. As she was doing so, the pastor of the church came in. He looked worried, harassed, almost ill.

"We have passed through such a desperate winter," he said, "desperate for everybody, Miss Franklin. Every once in a while I'm tired; every so often I get discouraged. But you always seem a dynamo of energy."

This was too much for Vera; she sat back from the typewriter and folded her hands in her lap. "I'm not a dynamo of energy," she said simply. "I'm just a human being like the rest of you and I get tired too. Do you know, I've had a big job offered me and I've half a mind to take it. The salary's more than double what I'm getting here and the work's easier and—" At sight of the expression upon the worn, middle-aged face of the pastor, her speech faltered.

The minister was staring at her strangely. "Somehow, Miss Franklin, I've grown to think of you as a fixture here. I love you like a daughter and I admire you as a helper. You've carried the cross along with all the rest of us in a gallant way! But if you want to leave, I won't stand in your way." All at once he sighed, and turned and walked out of the room. Vera was left alone with her thoughts, not knowing whether to be defiant or subdued.

In the midst of this mood she became aware of the tinkling sound of the telephone. She answered it and heard Richard Terry's voice coming clearly over the wire. "Miss Franklin," he said, without prelude, "I've been promoted. I'm to be manager of the whole chain of our factories now, not only of this factory. I want you to be the first to know it because now I can offer you even more than I offered you during our first interview."

Wildly, hysterically, Vera found that she was thinking of the fur coat, and that it was all tangled up with the minister's worried face and with Richard Terry's voice. "I'd like to talk to you again," she managed at last.

"Well, then," said Richard Terry, "meet me at lunch and we'll get things settled."

When Vera met Richard at the tea room around the corner from the parish house, she could not help noticing a tense sort of excitement about him.

They ate soup, creamed chicken, and salad. Richard Terry talked, boyishly, of his plans. They were plans that included all sorts of happy things: success, the home that he would one day own, motorcars, and trips to Europe. Vera did not say much. She had not time, for her companion's conversation filled every gap. At last, then, as they were eating their dessert, Richard came to the point.

"Well," he said, "it's time, Miss Franklin, that we got down to cases. Have you any encouragement to give me? I need help now as I've never needed it before. I've a big job to do, and I don't think I'll be able to do it alone."

Vera had come to the luncheon prepared to accept an important job. Now that the time had come, she found that she was regarding the young man who sat opposite with only misery in her eyes. It was because of the way he had said, "I'm not sure I'll be able to do it alone!" All at once she was remembering the pastor's tired face and the faces of the many other people who depended upon her—the poor ones, the sick ones, and the lonely ones. If a cheap, casual little typist came in, one who was not in sympathy with church work, who would help the pastor follow the way of the cross? Richard's use of the word *alone* had decided her.

"Oh," she half sobbed, "I came here to accept your offer, Mr. Terry. I really did. But I can't accept it, not now. I can't desert the people who need me. You can offer enough money to get the most efficient assistant in the world, but the church can't! With your future and your charm you can have anyone—and they can get only me!"

She stopped, for all at once Richard Terry had pushed aside the dessert dishes and was clasping her hand.

"I hoped you'd say just what you said, Miss Franklin—Vera," he whispered, "because I knew if you did, that you'd have proved to be what I thought you—the grandest, sweetest girl on this earth! Say, I have another job to offer you! Maybe you'll accept this one, even though it's for life. Maybe—"

His tone faltered and was lost, but his eyes held those of the girl. As she smiled an answer, she had entirely forgotten about fur coats and all other material things!

MARGARET E. SANGSTER JR. (1894–1981), *granddaughter of the equally illustrious Margaret E. Sangster Sr. (1838–1912), was born in Brooklyn, New York. Editor, scriptwriter, journalist, short-story writer, and novelist, she was one of the best-known and most beloved writers and editors of the twentieth century. She served as correspondent, columnist, and editor for David C. Cook and* Christian Herald Magazine, *and wrote books such as* Cross Roads *(1919),* The Island of Faith *(1921),* The Stars Come Home *(1936), and* Singing on the Road *(1936).*

FIFTEEN

A MATTER OF HONOR

William T. McElroy

This story saddens me. It saddens me because the Vance Carter in this story once represented the norm rather than a glaring exception in America. Not to have followed Carter's example would have been unthinkable to sons growing up in a society where both one's personal and family honor were held to be sacred.

Truly America can never be what it was until it once again regularly produces sons and daughters of the caliber of Vance Carter.

Mr. Clayton, president of the Greenvale National Bank, stared at his secretary, a puzzled expression on his face.

"What does this man look like?" he asked, running his thumb over the card she had just handed him. "Vance Carter died bankrupt two years ago. Yet this card bears his name."

"It may be his son, sir. It is a young man."

"Didn't remember that he had a son. Well, show him in; I'll see him."

A moment later a tall, calm-eyed young man stood in the presence of the banker.

"It was good of you to see me, sir," were his opening words. "You probably remember my father and his misfortunes. I've just finished college, and have come back to Greenvale to hunt a job and pay off the debts he left. I hoped you might need a man here in the bank."

The abrupt unexpectedness of the young man's statement took Banker Clayton off his guard for a moment.

"Er-er-yes, we do need a clerk. But let that stand for a moment. I remember your father, but I don't remember that he left any debts. He was forced unexpectedly into bankruptcy, wasn't he?"

"Yes sir. And it broke his heart. He gave up everything, even our home (mother had died years before), but all the sacrifices didn't quite clear up the indebtedness. He died within a month. I have had to work my last two years through college, but I've graduated now, and am ready to go to work, whenever I can get a job, to pay off the remaining indebtedness."

"But you don't owe anything," said the banker impatiently. "The courts settled the matter once and for all."

"I don't owe anything, *legally.* I understand that. But I'm not giving much consideration to that. *Morally* the debt stands. It's a matter of honor, you see, sir."

"Hm! Yes, I see. A matter of honor. How much was the indebtedness?"

"About five thousand dollars."

"And you have nothing?"

"Nothing but an education and willingness to work."

"Well, that's not a bad start. But, young man, the position we have open pays only thirty dollars a week. It'll take you a long time to save enough out of that to pay off five thousand dollars. You have to live, you know."

"Yes sir, but I'll live very inexpensively. Anyway, it's a start. Perhaps I may be able to make more money later on. I'll work hard. That debt must be paid sometime."

"When can you start to work?"

"Right now," was the prompt reply.

Thus it was that the vacancy in the clerical force at the Greenvale National Bank was filled. And it soon became evident that it was well filled. Mr. Clayton, whose curiosity had been aroused, kept a close watch over his new employee. The bank's force was composed of picked men, but none of them worked harder or more faithfully than the new clerk.

And none saved half so much in proportion to income. Out of his first paycheck Vance deposited half of the amount in the bank's savings department. So with the second, and the third, and so on, as President Clayton took pains to discover. How it was accomplished the bank president never could find out, though he argued with himself that it was the interests of the bank rather than personal curiosity that led him to investigate.

He found that the boy lived in a little room at the YMCA; that he denied himself most, if not all, of the ordinary pleasures of youth; and that to earn a little in addition to his salary he spent his evenings addressing envelopes for a circular letter company. Even so the bank president could not conceive of a young man of attractive personality as denying himself so uncomplainingly and persistently solely as "a matter of honor." He watched him closely, expecting to see him "break over," as he expressed it to himself, sooner or later.

But his expectations were doomed to disappointment. Vance did not "break over." As his salary increased, his savings account grew proportionately. At the end of three years he had three thousand dollars on deposit. In the seclusion of his private office Banker Clayton studied in quiet amazement the report a clerk had just placed before him.

"He's going to do it!" he exclaimed, slapping the desk with his open palm. "As I live, he's going to do it! He's the pluckiest chap I ever saw. For a son like that I'd give a million dollars and think I'd got a bargain."

Three more years passed. By this time Vance had become one of the most valued employees of the great banking institution. At last the day came toward which he had been working so long. As nearly as he could compute, he had money enough in the bank to meet the old debts in full and to pay interest on them at the regular legal rate. It was with a feeling of great relief and thankfulness that he sent out carefully worded invitations to all of his father's creditors to attend a dinner to be given a week or so later.

As he sealed and stamped the last envelope, he leaned back in his chair and took a deep breath. *I know now how a man feels who has just been let out of prison where he has been punished for something he did not do,* he told himself. *My! What a load is off my shoulders!*

For six years he had worked day and night to earn the money. Many an ambitious young man is willing to do that for himself. But to continue working so hard and denying himself so rigidly simply to satisfy a debt that the courts have decided one does not owe, is a different matter. But through the years he had worked and saved. Now he had reached the first of his life's goals—the satisfaction of all the claims that he felt were moral, even if not legal, obligations on him, and the clearing of his father's name as well. Now that the invitations were in the mail, another week would see the culmination of his long years of hard work and self-denying saving.

The next evening at a dinner party, from one of his friends who had received Vance's surprising note, President Clayton heard of the invitations. The following morning, in the midst of his duties, the clerk got a peremptory summons to come at once to the president's office. The banker looked up expectantly as the young man entered.

"Vance," he said, "I've heard of your dinner next week. I wonder if you'd consider me presumptuous if I asked for an invitation to it."

"No sir; I'd be glad to have you there."

"Well, I'll come on one condition. That is, that you will let me pay half the expenses of the dinner as a mark of my appreciation for what you are doing."

"I'm sorry, sir, but I can't do that."

"Why not?"

"Well, I guess it's just a matter of honor, sir."

"Hm! Still as keen as ever on these matters of honor, are you?"

"Yes sir, I hope so."

The shrewd bank president looked his clerk over for a long moment. After the silence and scrutiny had become embarrassing, he spoke again.

"Well, I'll come anyway—on your condition. I'll admit, Vance, though it's a sad admission for a man of my age, that I have a big lump of curiosity in this matter."

Vance grinned. "I'll be glad to have you come. I'd have invited you in the first place if I'd known you were interested."

"Interested! I didn't know such things ever happened outside of story books. I wouldn't stay away for a thousand dollars."

The information which Vance had given in his letters of invitation was sufficiently thrilling to those who had received them to bring practically a unanimous acceptance. There were further surprises awaiting the guests as they went to their places at the long table. Beneath the usual place cards each guest found at his plate an envelope containing an oblong slip of blue paper. There were none of these unopened two minutes after the men were seated. A hum of surprised conversation buzzed through the dining room, and many interested glances were turned in the direction of the quiet young man at the head of the table.

The dinner was a great success. It was not the quality of the food served, for Vance had not ordered an elaborate spread, but rather the unusual circumstances that had brought the group together. Probably the prevailing good humor could have been traced more particularly, if the truth were told, to the fact that each man present felt that he had found again a sum of money he had long ago charged off his books as gone forever.

There are few members of the human race who will not expand under such circumstances.

At last Vance shoved back his chair, and rapped on his water glass with a spoon to gain the attention of his guests. Amid the profound silence that ensued he began to speak. He reviewed briefly the circumstances of his father's heartbreaking failure in business.

Then he spoke even more briefly of his own struggles; of his resolution six years before to pay off the last cent of his father's debts; and how by hard work and careful saving he had come to this hour when he could present to every guest a check for the full amount of his loss, plus 6 percent interest for the entire period.

"It has not been easy," he concluded. "Of course, I knew that legally I owed nothing. That made it harder for me, when I grew discouraged, to go on. I admit that. But I feel sure my father would have fulfilled these obligations as a moral debt, had he lived; and I could do no less. From now on I can face the world, feeling that I have done my duty to my own conscience and to my father's memory. It has not been a legal matter to me; it has been rather, a matter of honor. I thank you for coming tonight as my guests. Whatever your pleasure has been this hour, I wish to assure you that mine has been greater."

As he ceased speaking, pandemonium broke loose. To an outsider it would have seemed more like a political convention than a gathering of dignified businessmen. Cheer after cheer rang through the room, and men almost climbed over each other to shake hands with their host.

When some semblance of order had been restored, Mr. Hillis, president of the great Hillis Manufacturing Company, began to speak. His words were to the effect that in a long business career this was the first time he had ever known such a thing to happen. But the point of his remarks, as he himself emphasized, was in his closing words.

"Greenvale should be proud to have such a citizen," he said. "And that no other town may be able to take him away from us, I wish in the presence of this company to offer him a position with my own firm at five thousand a year."

There was another outburst of cheering; but at last Mr. Clayton, who, through it all, had been trying to speak, succeeded in making himself heard above the din and shouting.

"Mr. Hillis is too late," he said with a smile, his hand on Vance's shoulder. "The Greenvale National Bank appreciates a man of honor too. Our board of directors at a special meeting at five o'clock this afternoon elected a new cashier. His salary is to be six thousand a year. And his name is Vance Carter."

That night before retiring, Vance took up his well-worn Bible. It had been his custom, since the days when as a little boy his mother had taught him the importance of reading his Bible every day, to read a few verses each night. As he opened the book, his eyes fell on a verse that had been heavily underscored some years before. It read, "Honor thy father and thy mother, that thy days may be long upon the land which the Lord thy God giveth thee."

WILLIAM T. McELROY *wrote for inspirational and family magazines during the first half of the twentieth century.*

SIXTEEN

CRUMPLED WINGS

John Scott Douglas

The nightmarish dream came back at him relentlessly: the fog, the propeller spinning off, the crash, and, of four people in the plane, he only surviving. Where was God in all this? What possible reason could there be for God's saving him rather than one of the other three?

It was in old Antigua, ancient capital of Guatemala, that the answer came.

The scene came back to Roy Baxter daily, almost hourly, like a horrible nightmare. It was a picture which blotted out all other pictures in his mind, all other scenes before his eyes. He had thought he might escape those ubiquitous memories in travel, only to learn to his sorrow that it is impossible to escape memories.

Now, in the palm-shaded patio of the *Casa de Mañana,* a hotel in Antigua, Guatemala, Roy listlessly ate a breakfast of huevos rancheros (eggs, rancher style) and drank black Guatemalan coffee. His lean brown face with its brooding blue eyes seemed years older than his twenty years as he stared at the splashing fountain in a setting of luxuriant flowers in the center of the stone patio. Then, in that strange way of late, his present surroundings faded into another scene.

He had been an airmail pilot on the New York–Chicago run, the youngest pilot, but one of the ablest. One night three passengers with political privileges presented themselves with orders from Washington which could not be ignored. Roy had explained that reports indicated fog in Pennsylvania's Himalayas, the Appalachian and Allegheny Mountains.

Roy remembered well his passengers. The man was a big jovial sort with smile lines connecting nose and mouth. He had laughed at Roy's suggestion of danger. The woman, his wife, was a sweet-faced person with countenance expressive of character and charm, reminding the youthful pilot of his own mother who had passed on. The girl, about Roy's age, possessed her mother's charm and had smiling, vivacious blue eyes.

They flew into that mountain fog on a moonless night—and they never flew out again. Roy remembered the horrible sensation of helplessness when the hub on the propeller flew off and the propeller followed it, robbing the airplane of all motive power. The propeller, spinning at nineteen hundred revolutions a minute, ripped through the lower wing of the biplane, nearly severing it. There he was, left as best he might to get them down, with his ship whose wings were fraying, whose motor he was forced to shut off to keep it from tearing itself and the airplane to pieces when the propeller flew off, and visibility nil.

Roy Baxter was no coward, but the terror of death was in his heart. Uttering a prayer that he could get his passengers down safely, regardless of what became of himself, he tried to glide to unseen crags below.

It was a hopeless "washout," of course. The miracle was that Roy Baxter lived and that the airplane and mail did not burn. The subsequent investigation completely exonerated him; no pilot could have done more than he had done to save his passengers. There was a recommendation that the type of airplane he had flown be discontinued in service because of radical structural and mechanical faults and that there be a limitation of passes issued on airmail planes.

An investigation, however, does not restore three lives. Roy Baxter was cleared of blame, and his position was open to him; but he could not go back. He explained matters to the "super" after the second trip, and was advised to lay off until he could forget.

Buying an airplane with his savings, he tried barnstorming for his living. Barnstorming required taking up passengers, however, and he was afraid of what might reoccur. Thinking distance might lessen the pain of memory, he flew down through Mexico and Guatemala, landing in Antigua. That ghastly scene still haunted him as it did now, however.

Why, of the four, wondered Roy, had he been the one to live? Was there any guiding hand to direct the destinies of man, to make order out of chaos? It did not seem so to him. He saw no reason why he, of the four, should have been spared! No supreme hand would have made such a decision. If humans just drifted through an aimless world like chaff in the wind, however, to what could he pin faith? This reasoning always led him back to the same futile question: Did anything really matter?

Roy's pondering mind was drawn from its own troubles by a rumbling and hissing. The young man glanced up at the three volcanoes which stood guardians over the ancient Spanish town of Antigua. They were called Agua, Fuego, and Acatenango. From the latter issued a plume of smoke, etched in black relief against the blue dome of the sky. Roy was indifferent to the fact that lava was now beginning to spill over the brim of the crater.

All the day before, smoke had issued from Acatenango in spurts, sometimes mushrooming five miles above the peak. Guatemalteco Indians in bright blue, red, and yellow homespun *huipiles* had trudged along the cobblestoned streets of the old town; others had departed in oxcarts containing their scanty possessions. Watching them, Roy was aware they sensed danger in the rumbling and growling of the volcano. Now that their Indian fears had materialized into reality, his instinct for self-preservation was still unaroused. *What does it matter, anyhow?* he asked himself.

Suddenly a car grated to a stop outside the hotel, and a man ran through the hardwood doors. He was a heavy, stolid-looking Guatemalteco with intelligent eyes and a strong jaw. Consternation was written in his phlegmatic features. "*Señor* Hans," he said breathlessly to the Dutch proprietor who sat at another table. "*Mi esposa! Mis niños!*" After exclaiming, "My wife! My children!" he broke into a series of excited Spanish words which Roy, knowing only fragments of the language, was unable to translate swiftly enough to comprehend.

The Dutch proprietor was first puzzled, then incredulous. He arose, walking to the center of the patio where he could better view the erupting volcano. For a moment he stood shading his light-blue eyes against the white glare of the sun; then he shrugged in characteristic Latin-American fashion. Roy heard him say, "Then nothing can save your wife and children."

For the first time in days something had seized the young man's interest. Roy risked an intrusion by asking, "What is wrong, *señor?*"

Hans Baer pointed a stubby, shaking finger at a lone adobe house on the side of the mountain. His gesture told Roy Baxter much of the story. This man had a hacienda on the side of Acatenango, taking advantage of the fertility of the incredibly rich volcanic soil. Now the octopus-like shadow had drawn black tentacles of lava about the hacienda on all sides, and was slowly closing about the house. It was impossible to reach this unfortunate man's abode.

"Surely your wife wouldn't stay there when the volcano started to erupt," said Roy, a crease furrowing his brow.

There was almost animation in the stolid face of the man as he said brokenly, "But, yes, *señor!* My wife would not leave! I went to Guatemala City two days ago on the bus, leaving my wife and two children, and I knew nothing of this! But she could not leave. My littlest child—my *niñito*—is so sick he cannot sit up. And my wife would not leave him, *señor.* It is not possible, *verdad?*"

Sudden emotion distorted the face of the young American, and something snapped in his brain. What folly to think life purpose-less; to wonder why he alone of those four in that airplane accident had survived! He knew the reason. Because he alone of those four had the ability to pay that debt of life to the world.

A warm feeling of security and strength seemed to flow in his veins at this realization. *Life was not meaningless! There was an understanding God who had worked out the intricate plan of lives.*

"I will save your wife and children," he cried suddenly. "I have a plane. If I can land in your garden, there may yet be hope—"

"It is madness!" exclaimed the plump proprietor of the *Casa de Mañana,* frowning. "You cannot land alive. And if you somehow managed to, how would you escape?"

Roy shrugged. "That I don't know. But something I *do* know is that a way will be shown me. I have faith in God. Everything is for a purpose. I came here, aimlessly, I thought, but in reality for the purpose of saving this man's wife and children. There is meaning in everything if we will listen to God's commands."

He hurried out to the cobblestoned street. The driver who had brought the *mozo* from Guatemala City was bargaining with a group of Guatemaltecos anxious to escape from Antigua. "You can come back here for them!" shouted Roy, jumping into the taxicab. "Take me to the landing field *muy pronto!*"

The driver nodded upon seeing the size of the fee Roy handed him, turned his car around, and went bumping across the uneven streets at a swift rate. Soon he drew up before the seldom-used landing field. Roy jumped out, darting across the field to his biplane.

He placed chocks before the wheels, primed his engine, and swung the "prop." On the third downward stroke the motor caught, bursting into a roaring song.

Leaping into the rear cockpit, Roy revved up the motor, meanwhile studying air, gas, and temperature gauges. Finally cutting the "gun," he adjusted his helmet and goggles, and then rocked the ship by quickly opening his throttle in jerky fashion until the biplane jumped its chocks and trundled down the undulating field.

The face of the pilot was grim and set behind his owl-like goggles. He jerked the control stick backward near the end of the field to bring up the nose. The little airplane wobbled free in space, climbing with motor roaring. Kicking the left rudder bar and easing his stick slightly to the left, Roy banked toward Acatenango, now belching black clouds of smoke.

The boiling slipstream hurled back hot ashes and cinders into his lean, resolute face, making breathing difficult. The biplane shuddered in the grip of conflicting wind currents caused by the frequent blasts of the volcano. Mud formed on his wings in great gray sheets as the stream mixed with the white ash filling the air.

As the biplane neared the mountain, Roy reasoned out his course. He saw one thing he had been unable to observe for certain from the *Casa de Mañana*. The reason the river of lava separated into two streams on either side of the adobe house was evident. A great point of rock above the house proved the point of cleavage. As the lava continued to flow, however, it was breaking new ground. In less than ten minutes it was probable the house would be surrounded by the incredibly hot molten stream.

Throwing his machine into a slow spin, Roy nosed down for the plowed ground behind the house. He wondered if he would survive the landing. He *must!* Loosening his safety belt as he neared the ground, he leveled out the biplane.

The airplane struck in what would have been a perfect three-point on level ground. Now, due to the rugged contour, the crate bumped along unevenly for a dozen feet, nosed up, and sent Roy catapulting forward as it did so. When he staggered to his feet, some distance from the plane, it had pivoted over on one wing, which was crumpled beneath the twisted mass of wreckage.

Something constricted in his throat. His hope of taking the woman and two children out in his airplane was shattered.

A short woman with toil-worn face came rushing toward Roy. *"Señor! Señor!"* she exclaimed. "Are you hurt?"

He forced a pale smile to his lips. "No," he answered her in Spanish; "but I'm afraid we're all in a bad way. I'd hoped to take you out in my plane."

Fear and despair looked out of her eyes as she surveyed the twisted heap of metal, wood, and fabric.

Roy stared with narrowed eyes at the stream of lava already striking the edge of the house. He turned his eyes to the great natural barrier of rock which had so far cleaved the stream. "Quick!" he muttered thickly. "We must run toward the big rock. It's our only hope!"

Roy sprang toward the house. A girl was crying on the floor. "Go to your mother!" he directed her tersely in Spanish. On the bed lay a boy with flushed brown cheeks and fever-bright eyes. This was the *niñito* of whom the *mozo* had spoken; sick with malaria, Roy guessed.

He picked up the boy in his arms, hurrying to the door. A thin, black stream had already trickled through the doorway. Roy leaped over it, staggering, and hurried on up the slope to the place where the mother was standing as he had left her, her mind evidently still numb from the hopelessness of her position. "Come," he said hoarsely. She followed him up the precipitous slope like a child, the girl clinging to her hand.

The air was stifling, stagnant with the fumes of the volcano, and Roy panted from the burden of the sick child in his arms. His airplane was burning now, ignited by the river of lava which had surrounded the house. He had arrived just in time. As he looked ahead, Roy wondered if, even so, he had not been too late. The path was growing narrower.

The woman sobbed. "We can't make it, *señor.* It's hopeless!"

"Have faith," said Roy, through clenched teeth. "Trust in God."

He staggered on, the stream seemingly closing after them to shut off escape to the rear, should they be mad enough to attempt it. The adobe house was crumbling. One wall tottered and fell inward as Roy gave one hasty backward glance.

The path ahead narrowed to a yard—two feet—a foot—and then in places to a space barely permitting passage. Roy staggered on, great drops of perspiration pouring down his face at the exertion.

At last they reached the great outthrust boulder which clove the stream of lava. Spent with their climb, the mother and the girl lay panting on the hot rock. Roy laid the little invalid beside him, and watched with a grim sort of satisfaction as the trail closed behind them.

Hours dragged on, and the convulsions of the volcano grew less frequent. Roy knew they were saved. He knew, too, that he had been saved from a life of futility by the realization of that day. He would return to his position with the New York–Chicago mail line because that would be the hardest thing to do. He had been running away from duty. It would be a pleasant duty if he would but remember that it was his only way of repaying God for giving him that opportunity to serve man.

JOHN SCOTT DOUGLAS *was one of the most prolific writers of adventure stories during the first half of the twentieth century. He specialized in stories dealing with early aviation.*

SEVENTEEN

WAR ON YELLOW FEVER

Ruth Fox

The classic symptoms were all too well known: "frightful pains in the arms and legs, yellowness of the skin and eyeballs, bleeding in the stomach, high fever—and, usually, the delirious death." In war, yellow fever slew many more men than the guns ever did. What wasn't known was what caused it.

Who would be crazy enough to ask for almost certain death in order to find out? After all, being a hero would be small consolation if the process of becoming one killed you.

———

Leaning on the ship's railing, the captain waved a beefy hand and said, "There she is, Major Reed! Greatest sight in the world, and I've seen them all!"

The sight was Havana harbor. Major Walter Reed, who was seasick, also thought the sight the greatest in the world. And dry land would have seemed great. He clutched the railing of the ship and averted his eyes from the dizzily rolling coastline.

"Wouldn't live any place but Cuba—that is, if I ever lived in any place longer'n a week," the captain announced, laughing uproariously for reasons which escaped the pallid major.

"Too many bugs for my liking," said Walter Reed, slapping at a mosquito on his wrist.

The captain raised his eyes eloquently, as though he were calling for heavenly patience, and said, "Few little mosquitoes never hurt a grown man yet. Why, Major, they're part of the scenery, and—"

Walter Reed, blinking into the sun-streaked coastline, interrupted him. "Isn't that a fire in the harbor?" he asked.

"Probably another yellow-jack cargo being burned," replied the captain, glancing casually in the direction indicated. "The way the epidemic is spreading, we have enough yellow fever here right now without importing it!"

Although in 1900 the sight of a ship's cargo being burned on suspicion of yellow fever was not so common as it had been twenty years before, it was by no means a novelty, particularly in times of epidemic. And an epidemic was currently raging throughout Cuba.

"How were things when you left?" Walter Reed inquired.

"There was a fresh outbreak in the barracks, and the fever was spreading like wildfire. Same old story. It's a great pity that there's no way to stop yellow jack, Major. It kills thousands wherever it strikes. But all the doctors can do is burn up bedding, and keep their fingers crossed, and after that—"

A hail from the quarterdeck interrupted him. He shouted back an order and then said, "See you ashore, Major. Hope you enjoy your stay, and don't let our bugs bother you. Remember, mosquitoes are harmless. Tourists like 'em!" He stamped off, bellowing additional advice to the quarterdeck. Reed sighed with relief, then winced as the cross currents of the channel bounced the ship.

In the self-pitying mood which always accompanies seasickness, he severely doubted that he could do the job he had been sent down to Cuba to do. He had been sent as head of a four-man army commission appointed to investigate the unknown causes of yellow fever.

Yellow fever had struck the United States eighty-six times between 1668 and 1900. In Memphis, the epidemic of 1878 killed five thousand people in two weeks and drove thirty thousand more out of the stricken city.

About the time of the 1878 epidemic doctors began to believe that yellow fever occupied a peculiar place between contagious and noncontagious diseases. It was not spread by direct contact like smallpox, they said, for the "emanations" from the sick required a warm, dark place in which to grow strong enough to infect the next comer. The sick man himself was harmless. But his bedding, his clothing, his furniture, any of his material possessions, in fact—these were the villains. The term *fomites*—a Latin word meaning substances which could transmit contagion—came into use.

Let a ship from a town even remotely suspected of infection drop anchor in any harbor, and its cargo was immediately dumped on the wharf and burned. The cargo was no longer cargo. It had become fomites. The wholesale destruction of the personal property of yellow fever victims was almost certain.

The fomites theory seemed the only way to explain the strange way in which the disease spread. It could hardly be said to spread at all. It jumped. "It often leaves a block or house intact," wrote one observer in 1878, "going around it and attacking those beyond. A thin board partition seems to have stopped it on Governor's Island in 1856. And it once attacked the sailors in all the berths on one side of a ship before crossing to the other. Such odd instances, in the present state of our knowledge, are impossible to explain."

And now Walter Reed and three other doctors, James Carroll, Aristides Argamonte, and Jesse Lazear, were supposed to find the cause of yellow fever.

Soon after Reed's arrival in Havana he met with the other three men, and they set up a program of laboratory research. But before their program was well underway, the doctors were asked to look in on the Pinar del Rio post, a hundred miles from Havana, where some sort of tropical fever was raging. Yellow fever? No one was quite sure. Reed and Argamonte traveled to the army post, did a few autopsies, and took a long look around.

Reed had strange conclusions to report to Carroll and Lazear the next day. "Thirty-five men are in the hospital," he said. "Eleven dead. All unmistakable cases of yellow fever." He looked to Argamonte for confirmation.

Argamonte, as a native Cuban, had seen a lot of yellow fever. He nodded. Yellow fever was not hard to diagnose. There were only too many classic symptoms: frightful pains in the arms and legs, yellowness of the skin and eyeballs, bleeding in the stomach, high fever—and, usually, the delirious death.

"Unmistakable cases," Reed repeated. "But the new staff at the post hospital didn't recognize the disease as yellow fever. Consequently no one at the hospital paid any attention to the bedding of those men. Nothing was burned. There was no special disinfecting of their sheets, their mattresses, or their clothing. But—" he paused empathetically, "did any of the nurses, or the people in the laundry, or the other patients pick up yellow jack from the stuff? Not one. Eight barracks were full of contaminated clothes. That stuff should have had enough fomites in it to infect anyone who came within ten feet. But not one—not one single man in any of those eight barracks—caught anything."

"They were immune?" Carroll inquired cautiously.

"No. None of them has had it before. The question is, why haven't they got it now? And where did it come from in the first place?"

"There's an old man on this island," Lazear said, "who would tell you that it flew in the window on the wings of a female mosquito. Carlos Finlay has been saying that for quite a few years."

"In Cuba," Argamonte said, "it's hard to remember a time when old Finlay wasn't saying it."

"It makes as much sense as the fomites theory," observed Carroll.

"How do the people down here feel about Finlay's ideas?" Reed asked after a few seconds' thought.

Argamonte shrugged. "Very few people pay any attention to him."

"Maybe he's on the right track," Reed said suddenly. "Did any of you ever read a paper by an army surgeon named Henry Carter? About yellow fever transmission?"

"Is Carter the one who kept records of how yellow fever spread in the Mississippi epidemic?" asked Lazear.

Reed nodded. "Carter found that there was an unexplained time lapse between the first reported case and the outbreak of a number of cases. Two or three weeks might pass before a second person developed any symptoms of the disease. But after that, a rash of victims would be stricken all at once."

He paused a moment, thinking, then went on excitedly. "Suppose that a yellow fever victim—just one—is brought into town, on a ship, for example. Suppose that a passing mosquito bites the victim and draws the yellow fever germ into her stomach. Suppose that the germ incubates and is carried some days later to the salivary glands of the mosquito. From here on, everyone the mosquito bites can catch the disease."

It now became clear that the claims of Dr. Finlay were due for some first-class investigation. Proving the mosquito-transmission theory was, in principle, a simple matter. One would simply allow a mosquito to bite a yellow fever victim, have the same mosquito bite a healthy man, and then sit back and wait for him to get yellow fever. But how could the commission take such a chance with human life? Walter Reed felt that it was his business to save lives, not to sacrifice them by trying to prove an idea that hadn't been demonstrated satisfactorily.

The other three men were less tender-hearted. Hundreds of thousands of people, they pointed out, had already died of yellow fever. What difference did it make if a few more got it or even died of it, if by so doing they could put an end to the business once and for all? In the recent war with Spain, only 862 men had been killed in battle, and 106 had died of wounds. But 5,438 people had died of diseases—typhoid and yellow fever leading the list.

All this made sense, but it did not bring about Reed's decision to use human guinea pigs. The clinching argument was that yellow fever could not, at the time, be produced in animals. Therefore human beings must be infected with it. No matter how delicate the conscience of a researcher, he could arrive at no other conclusion. Volunteers would have to be called for; but the first volunteers, the commission decided, would be the commission itself.

While they were making their initial plans, Reed had to return to the States on medical business. He promised to return as quickly as possible, leaving the others to begin Operation Mosquito.

First they allowed their laboratory-bred insects to feed, one by one, on the blood of yellow fever patients. Lazear had charge of the brood of mosquitoes. He kept each of them in its own gauze-stoppered jar, each jar labeled with the date on which the mosquito had bitten a patient and the stage of the disease at the time.

Dr. Lazear made the first experiment on himself. Agramonte,

to his own annoyance, was immune, having had the disease in childhood. The technique was simple. Lazear lured the mosquito into a test tube, inverted the tube over his arm, tapped the bottom of the glass to call the attention of the creature to the treat at the other end, and let her bite. That was all there was to it.

To Dr. Lazear's disgust, he didn't get yellow fever. Could he be naturally immune? Or had his mosquitoes been too recently infected to pass along the disease? He wondered.

On August 27 Lazear took Dr. Carroll into the laboratory and showed him a mosquito which he considered the prize of his collection. The insect had bitten not one but four yellow fever patients, the first of them twelve days ago. The cases had ranged from very mild to very severe. If any mosquito of his brood was ripe for action, Lazear asserted, this was it.

"Let's give her a chance to show off," Carroll said, observing the innocent-looking insect curiously through his rimless glasses.

Lazear's handsome face was solemn. "You're sure you want to try?"

"Didn't you?"

Lazear smiled. "And what happened? Nothing."

"Well, better luck next time. Here. Let her out." Carroll rolled up his sleeve and thoughtfully watched the mosquito as she slid down the tube and lighted on his arm. The night after, he wrote to Reed. "If there is anything in the mosquito theory," he said, "I should get a good dose."

He did. In fact, for three days his recovery was doubtful. Lazear was frantic with worry. Of course he had done what he set out to do. He had produced the first experimental case of yellow fever by the bite of a mosquito. But had he killed his friend in the process? Almost, but not quite. Slowly Carroll began to rally, and soon he was out of danger.

Their fear at rest, Lazear and Agramonte considered the situation. Carroll's yellow fever showed that they were on the right track.

Further success came when Lazear allowed one of his mosquitoes to bite another volunteer, referred to in their reports as Case XY (actually a young private named William Dean). Case XY also contracted the disease, but he threw it off with less difficulty than the forty-six-year-old Carroll had done.

Two cases of mosquito transmission! Lazear's heart was filled with strange affection for his brood. Reed would be back soon and then things would really start popping! The young man's head was buzzing with ideas for procedure and practice. He was more sure than any of them that they would soon see their theory turned into undeniable fact. A week later he was dead of one of the worst yellow-fever cases the hospital had ever seen.

When Reed returned in October, he found the shadow of Lazear's fate lying heavily over the camp. He himself was so saddened by the tragedy that even the promised success of their mission could produce no emotion in him at all. How had it happened? he asked.

"A mosquito bit him while he was making the ward rounds," Carroll said. "He said he noticed it, but he didn't think it was the right kind of a mosquito and he let it stay on his hand. He told me about it the day he got sick."

Their first enthusiasm gone, Reed, Carroll, and Agramonte got back to work. They had two cases to work with, but one of them, Carroll's, was not considered conclusive by anyone but himself. He had, after all, been exposed to all the yellow fever in the hospital for weeks. How did anyone know that the mosquito bite had anything to do with his attack?

But Mr. XY was something else again. He had been in the hospital at Camp Columbia for two months, and there was no yellow fever at Camp Columbia. Lazear's mosquito had been the only source of infection to which he had been exposed.

On the basis of his present knowledge, Reed took two decisive steps. He wrote a paper to be read at an American Health Association meeting in which he stated definitely that the mosquito acts as the carrier of yellow fever. And he applied to the military governor of Cuba for enough money to carry out one large-scale piece of research, so perfectly controlled that not even the most violent anti-mosquito, pro-fomites men could quarrel with the results.

He was granted the money, and he set up Camp Lazear, which became the official testing ground of the commission. While the station was in the planning stages, Reed worried over one vital point. Since Lazear's death and Carroll's near escape, the work of the commission, taken lightly at first, had been regarded with greater and greater awe by the American soldiers and the natives alike. The experimental station would soon be ready, but would there be anyone around on whom to experiment? Reed himself was the only member of the board left who was not immune. He was anxious to try one of the mosquitoes on himself, but it was not practical to do so until he was sure that operations at the camp were running smoothly. Fifty-year-old men, he knew, did not make quick recoveries from yellow fever, assuming that they recovered at all.

The military governor of Cuba had promised to pay volunteers for their services, and this information was spread through the barracks and among the native population. The day after the news made the rounds of Camp Columbia, Reed was visited in his office by two young men—John Moran and John Kissinger. They had heard about the major's need for volunteers in the yellow-fever tests, they said. They would be willing to help out.

Reed was amazed. These two men, about the age of his own son, were hospital corpsmen. They knew yellow fever. He said, "I admire your courage, boys. I know that you both understand exactly what you're letting yourselves in for."

They nodded.

"In any case" he went on, "I'm glad that we can pay you a little something for your services. It's not much, considering. But—one hundred dollars if you don't get yellow jack; two hundred if you do. We—"

"Major," Morgan interrupted, "we weren't figuring on anything like that. In fact," he added more decisively, "we wouldn't want to do it if we had to take money for it."

This time Reed was really taken aback. He said, "But you—suppose that—" He stopped and studied their faces briefly. "Are you sure that's the way you feel about it?"

"Yes sir," Kissinger said. "We don't care about the money. But we thought that—" He flushed slightly. "We thought we'd like to do something for humanity and science." Moran nodded, solemn-faced.

Reed sighed, touched both by their spirit and by their naive expression of it. He said simply, "Gentlemen, I salute you." Of these two he wrote later, *In my opinion, the moral courage of these young men has never been surpassed in the history of the United States Army.*

Camp Lazear was just an open field on which seven tents were pitched and two small houses were built. The permanent personnel at this camp numbered fifteen. Three of them were the remaining members of the commission; three more were staff men known to be immune to yellow fever.

No one could come into Camp Lazear but its immune members; its non-immune members could leave whenever they cared to, but once they went out they could never return. All the people inside were known to be free from yellow-fever infection at the time the experiments began. Nor were there any mosquitoes on the well-drained, windy field except the specially bred laboratory insects trapped in the commission's test tubes. As of December 5, 1900, at two o'clock in the afternoon, Camp Lazear was the one spot in Cuba absolutely guaranteed to be safe from yellow fever.

Agramonte, stationed at the yellow-fever hospital in Havana, was in charge of mosquito-infecting. He had an inexhaustible source of supply. Agramonte himself transferred the insects from the hospital to the camp, his pockets bulging with test tubes. Once in camp, the bugs were removed to artificially warmed quarters and were coddled and catered to. No other mosquitoes in history had ever been so pampered.

Kissinger was the first of the volunteers to be bitten. His partner in the experiment was a mosquito that had sucked the blood of a yellow-fever patient eleven days before The camp waited, no one more eagerly than Kissinger, for the incubation period to pass. The camp noted, no one more regretfully than Kissinger, that he remained in roaring good health. A second try, with the same mosquito, produced no results whatsoever on Kissinger. The mosquito herself died three days later.

"What do you think it is, Major Reed?" the soldier asked him one day, after a quick check had shown his pulse to be seventy-two, his temperature 98.6, and his blood pressure 120. "Do you think I'm immune?"

"Not necessarily. We have a new idea on the incubation period required now that the weather's colder. Let's try it again. This time we'll really do the job right. Five mosquitoes—they all bit yellow-fever cases over two weeks ago."

"Anything you say, Major," the boy agreed, grinning broadly. He added hopefully, "Wait and see! I'll get yellow jack this time if it kills me!"

Reed winced. It had not been the happiest choice of words.

Three days later Kissinger was exhibiting all the symptoms of yellow fever. He was removed to the hospital and every local yellow-fever authority was invited to come in and look at him.

It was a good case—unmistakably yellow fever, but mild enough to make recovery certain. It was all that the camp could have asked. None of the visiting physicians disputed the diagnosis. And no one was happier with the results than Kissinger himself.

While Kissinger had been waiting to be stricken, another sort of experiment was under way at the camp. Proving that the female mosquito spread yellow fever was only half the job. Proving that fomites did *not* transmit the disease was the other half. Orders passed from Reed to the hospital in Havana, and some days later three mysterious wooden boxes were delivered to Camp Lazear. They were deposited in one of the small houses which had been built at the camp.

It was an ugly little shack, fourteen by twenty feet in size, its walls two boards thick, its windows heavily screened and shuttered. A double-doored hall admitted one to this unpleasant little home which came equipped with a coal-oil stove and a temperature of ninety degrees. Building Number One, as it was called, contained nothing but the stove, three army cots, and now the mysterious crates from the hospital. A volunteer doctor and two hospital corps privates went into the house and broke open the crates.

For two weeks the boxes had been packed tight with soiled linen and blankets from the yellow-fever hospital. Special pains had been taken in the packing of these boxes. Not just ordinarily dirty linen would do. The sheets had to be caked stiff with the thick black liquid which gave the disease its popular name, *el vomito negro* (Spanish for "black vomit").

The three men dumped the contents of the boxes onto the

floor, then shook out each object thoroughly, in order to "spread" the fomites with which the mess was supposed to be loaded. The first shock of the repulsive odor was too much for them and, to a man, they dashed for the door of the horrible little house, gasping for fresh air. The impulse to shake the dust of Camp Lazear from their feet must, at that moment, have been as overpowering as the stench in Building Number One. But they went back inside. They had volunteered for the fomites experiment and they would stay with it. And if any fomites in the world could produce yellow fever, these were the fomites to do it.

They made up the beds with the linen and blankets, crawled in between the sheets and waited for morning. It was not even to be imagined that they slept. The next morning they were conducted to the quarantined tent where they were to spend their days for the duration of the experiment.

This was on November 30. Until December 19, twenty-one days later, the three men returned to their nauseous house with each sunset and stayed there until morning.

"Hey, fellows," the immune soldier who brought them their food announced one day. "Kissinger has yellow jack—from a mosquito. He's been sent to the hospital."

One of the inmates looked bored. "Private Kissinger," he announced to his companions, ceremoniously turning to address them, "has yellow jack—from a mosquito."

"Poor fellow. Imagine having to go to that nice clean hospital," one of the others said, clucking sympathetically. "Do extend our good wishes to Private Kissinger and tell him that if he can think of any way in which we could replace him, we would be only too happy."

"Well, after all," the messenger said, somewhat taken aback, "if mosquitoes *do* spread yellow fever, then maybe fomites *don't* and you fellows are safe."

"At this point, son, a nice case of yellow fever would be a plea-sure—an absolute joy!" the first private announced pleasantly.

"But—"

"You wouldn't understand. Pass along, old friend, and don't disturb our thoughts. We only have twenty-four hours a day to think, you know."

On December 19 the three heroes were released from further dealings with fomites and were observed under quarantine for five days. After that they were allowed the run of the camp, not a flushed face or a racing pulse among them.

Two more volunteers took up nightly residence in Building Number One, under similar conditions, but with an added touch. These men wore the very pajamas that had belonged to yellow-fever victims. And twenty days later they were succeeded by two others who slept on pillowcases soaked in the blood of assorted yellow-fever victims.

Of the whole experiment Reed wrote simply, *The attempt which we have made to infect Building Number One and its seven non-immune occupants during a period of sixty-three days has proved an absolute failure.* What the seven non-immune occupants might have said to anyone who ever suggested to them afterward that fomites convey yellow fever would probably make stimulating reading.

The second house at Camp Lazear was similar to Building Number One in size, but in no other way. It was well ventilated; it was furnished with nothing but steam-disinfected articles; its bedding was sterile; its residents were sent in fresh from long, soapy baths. It was the sort of place that must have haunted the dreams of the men who were living in Building Number One.

Building Number Two was divided in the middle by a sheet of fine wire net, but its windows were arranged to ensure good cross-ventilation. Into one side of the building were released fifteen hungry mosquitoes. Shortly after, they were joined by John Moran, the second of Reed's two volunteers. At the same time, two other non-immune soldiers entered the other side of the house and watched through the mosquito-proof wire while the mosquitoes went to work on Private Moran. Three times that day, Moran returned to the house for the purpose of being bitten by the contaminated insects. Four days later—on Christmas day—Moran had a fever of 104.2. The other occupants of the building remained in excellent health.

The filthy, reeking houseful of fomites had done no harm to anyone. In the antiseptic dwelling next door, a man had caught yellow fever. The case was proved beyond a shadow of a doubt.

These clean-cut experiments, backed by the authority of the United States Army, brought about a quick acceptance of the commission's findings. Walter Reed's research team had produced the facts. A group of sanitation experts made use of them, and by September of 1901 there was not a single case of yellow fever left in Havana.

Walter Reed's successful war against yellow fever represents one of the greatest medical triumphs of the human race. But whenever the human race becomes obsessed with its own cleverness, it might remind itself that four hundred years, hundreds of thousands of lives, millions of dollars, a rare collection of scientific brilliance, and the United States Army, were required before man could get ahead of the mosquito.

RUTH FOX *wrote for popular magazines during the first half of the twentieth century.*

EIGHTEEN

HULDAH DEANE'S HEROISM

Mrs. M. S. Peters

Oh, to be able to make a difference! To be able to go out in a lifeboat and help to save those about to drown!

Why, she'd rather be that swooping osprey than a useless girl like herself! This story is 120 years old, and apparently is a true account.

A sky darkened by clouds hurrying before driving winds, a sea gray-faced and wrinkled tossing restlessly beneath a mass of barren rocks upon which stood a tall lighthouse, made up the dreary picture Huldah Deane was gazing upon with such wistful intentness. Her gray eyes presently followed the swoop of an osprey and his after-flight upward with his prey in his talons.

"I would rather be that fish hawk than Huldah Deane," she said, giving expression to her gloomy thoughts. "I must stay here day in, year out—here, where nothing happens, where the sea frets, and I fret with it. So I light the captain's pipe, scrub the tower, and do chores for the dame. Who cares what else I do, or what becomes of me? Yes, old sea, I'd rather be a fish hawk, and snatch fish from you, than be Huldah Deane. Oh dear! If something would only happen! If I could do something great or wonderful—go out in a lifeboat, maybe, to save drowning folks, or—"

"Huldy! Huldy Deane!" The quick, impatient call reached her, even above the roaring of the surf. It was Captain Dutton's voice. "Come right on, quick! Mother's taken in a spell an' I can't make it out."

Huldah obeyed in awed silence. *A spell the captain couldn't make out must be very bad,* she thought. What if neither she nor anybody else could make it out? And, alas! Who could understand the fixed stare of the dame's kind eyes, or the pinched shrinking of the features so suddenly grown unfamiliar to the two who dwelt under the same roof with her?

"She's got to hev the doctor as soon as he can be fetched, Huldy."

"The doctor from shore?" questioned the girl.

"Certain. There's none closer as I know. Do you?"

"No," she gravely answered; "but the mainland's a long ways off, and a storm's rising."

"It makes no difference," said Captain Dutton, stubbornly. "She's been a good mother to me, an' she's in a bad fix. The doctor's got to be fetched, that's all."

In his rough, good-hearted way the captain loved his mother as he loved nothing else.

"Ef she should die, I'd want her to know somehow as I tried to do my duty by her to the last. And, Huldy"—laying his hand on the girl's shoulder—"I ain't concerned but what she'll be took care of as fur as you can do it, child. It's hard to leave a young one like you here with such terrible trouble, but there's no help for it. I'll fetch the doctor soon as I kin—leastways 'fore the sun drops. No sailor kin say as ever Kyle Dutton missed lightin' the beacon wi' the last ray o' sunshine, or turnin' off lamps as the sun stepped 'crost the horizon. Livin', I'll be here in time for that, Huldy."

He nodded and went away.

Huldah shivered as she glanced down at the motionless figure on the couch. Maybe she would be left thus utterly alone for hours—for days. Her breath came hurriedly. It seemed to her more than she could bear. Frantically she forced open the window, and, thrusting her head through, shouted herself hoarse in a vain effort to make Captain Dutton hear her above the roaring of the sea. The boat, tossed from wave to wave, plunged further and further away.

And it was but a few hours before that Huldah had wished she might have an opportunity to do some great heroic deed. Now she said to herself: *You were a pitiful coward then, Huldah Deane. You brave enough to go in a lifeboat to save drowning folks! You deserve to be nothing better than a fish hawk. Because Dame Dutton lies ill yonder, and the captain puts off to fetch a doctor, is that any reason why you should go into spasms of fright? For shame! Remember what Father told you that day he sailed away, never to come back any more: "Do your duty always, Huldah." Isn't it your duty now, foolish girl, to get right down from here and see to poor Mrs. Dutton?*

Closing the window, she descended from her perch to renew her exertions for the relief of the poor woman. But toil as she might, nothing she did could change the fixed attitude, or calm the quick-drawn breath that told of bitter suffering.

Sometime later, the day began to wane. The clouds ranged themselves in solid masses, and darkness and storm besieged the sea-girt tower. Crossing to the clock in the corner, she scanned its face. "Five o'clock! So late? Why, the sun will be down in less than half an hour, and the captain will lose his position if the beacon is not lighted by sundown. But what can I do? It's the order, he says, that women and children shan't have anything to do with the lights."

One moment she stood with tightly compressed lips. Then a brave, resolute smile parted those lips.

"Well, I'm hardly a child, I suppose, but neither am I a woman. Ships may be lost if the beacon is not lit." Then lighting the lantern the captain always used, she hung it on her arm, and after one more look at the sick woman, left the chamber.

Almost at the threshold began the seemingly endless stairway, winding up into regions of height and loneliness. She didn't allow herself to hesitate now, but began the ascent hurriedly. A fearful journey it seemed through the darkness, broken only by fitful glimmerings of her lantern and, now and then, cross rays of light from the slits of windows in the thick walls. Clasping the iron rail, she toiled on, her strength failing, her heart thumping, and her brain in a whirl. Not until she had reached the top step did she drop down to rest. Exhausted by fatigue and nervous excitement, she had to recover strength before she could even open the door into the lantern room.

Fortunately the great lamps were trimmed and supplied with oil. Every part of the machinery was also in working order. Captain Dutton was one of the most careful of the lighthouse keepers.

"And he'll see that I don't intend for him to lose his position because of just one night's failure to light the tower," Huldah said, her heart warming for the first time to the silent man who had, in his way, done his duty by her as well as by the place of trust he filled. "Who knows, though, this light may fall upon the very spot where he has gone down to the bottom of the sea."

Again a shiver crept over the slender figure, and only the blazing forth of the beacon dispelled her vivid fancy. One by one the

lamps flared up, and were turned into place. The reflectors, pol-
ished to their utmost, caught the cheerful rays and sent them in a
far-reaching circle of radiance out through the darkness and the
storm, to give warning to those who were "gone down to the sea
in ships."

But this was only the beginning of Huldah's work. It was a
chief part of the keeper's duty, she knew, to see that the lights
burned undimmed throughout the night. Now, however, she must
return to attend to the woman below. But as she turned to go there
was a sudden crashing of the glass above her, a whirring swoop of
some swift-winged creature overhead, a gust of wind, a flaring of
the circle of lights, and then darkness—rayless, absolute. The storm
moaned and shrieked in her ears, and Huldah shrieked too, hiding
her face in her shawl.

What had happened? Again the winged intruder whirred by,
beating the air with wearied and dripping plumage. Ah! Now she
understood. Once Captain Dutton had told her of a storm bird
breaking one of his transparencies. Attracted by the light, doubt-
less, the wanderer had dashed against the glass.

There was but one thing to be done. She could not hope to re-
light the lamps until those blasts were shut out. She must find
another frame and transparency.

How the long descent was accomplished Huldah could never
think afterward without a shudder. At the very outset, when
she had groped her way to the landing, and had succeeded in re-
lighting her little lantern, the door she had latched behind her flew
open, giving outlet to those terrible winds, which tore at her clothing savagely, extinguishing her light, and leaving her again in darkness. Of necessity she stood still until the currents had strangled each
other and sunk down into the depths of gloom below her. Then,
shutting her eyes tightly, she continued on her perilous journey.

From the basement stores she procured the frame and fixtures, and returning with them by the same winding route upward, found it not such a difficult thing to unhinge and replace the shattered transparency, the tempest having lulled slightly, and the force of the wind being broken. Yet by the time her task was complete, and the lamps re-lit, her strength failed her. Vaguely thinking that maybe she was going to die, she collapsed upon the floor, and with a deep-drawn sigh she closed her eyes.

———

Four hours later an Inspector from the mainland passing to the island lighthouse was hailed by the captain of a brig which had weathered the storm and come to anchor for repairs.

"What ails the tower light, sir?" he asked of the officer, nodding toward the beacon, through the transparencies of which a steady stream of light was still pouring, though the sun was doing his best to dim its glory.

The Inspector frowned. "I only know that the keeper's neglecting his duty."

The sailor shook his head. "Something more's amiss, I'm thinking. The light come near playing us a jack-o'-lantern trick just before day. She put on her nightcap all of a sudden, and 'twas like the polestar had let loose o' the compass needle. A little more'n we'd 'a dashed upon the reefs, only she waked up and showed us her shiners. And not a wink has she took since. Somewhat's wrong. Cap'n Dutton's been prompt as the sun this twenty year."

"Captain Dutton? Is't Captain Kyle Dutton that's keeper of the lighthouse yonder?" asked one of the brig's passengers, starting forward, excitedly.

"Yes, Kyle Dutton. He's an odd chap, but he ain't the fellow to shirk duty."

In a moment the stranger had asked to be put ashore.

The landing was effected with little risk, but those of the boat's crew who ascended the cliff and sought entrance to the tower found themselves baffled. The ladder was gone, the iron door barred, and all their pounding awoke no response other than muffled echoes from the interior.

"We may get in through a window," said the Inspector. "Hodges, fetch the boat hook."

The hook was brought, and at the second throw caught over the iron balcony under Dame Dutton's window.

The Inspector climbed the rope, followed by the others, and soon admission was gained to the room beneath.

"Here's one of the Seven Sleepers," said Dick Trail, going up to the couch. He started back. "Why, it's the Cap'n's mother, and she looks as if she were dying."

Two of the men gathered closer to see what they could do for the poor woman, and the others began to search the tower. No clue to the mystery, if mystery it contained, was found below. Together in silence they mounted the long winding stairway.

A flood of mellow light poured upon the group as the officer opened the door into the lantern room. There upon the floor, bathed in the glory of light, lay Huldah Deane. To her locked senses, lulled into unconsciousness by the roar of the storm-lashed ocean, the tumult in the tower had never reached.

She was only awakened now by feeling herself lifted in a pair of strong arms, and strained to the breast of the stranger seaman.

"Huldah! Huldah! My little one! My daughter!" she heard a tender voice murmuring, and in her glimmer of consciousness felt his tears dropping on her face.

After the first wild emotion of joy, what a sense of rest the child had, feeling the protecting arms of her father about her! For the stranger, who had endured shipwreck and danger, was none other than Huldah's father.

With only the name of Kyle Dutton, who had taken Huldah from the orphanage where he had placed her before sailing on his last ill-fated voyage to furnish him a clue, Captain Deane, after a vain search of months, had been guided into the presence of his child by the beacon her little hands had lighted.

There were honest tears in the eyes looking upon this reunion; neither did one of those strong hearts fail to respond with a thrill of admiration as the daughter recounted to her father the trials to which her fortitude and courage had been subjected during the past night of tempest and awful solitude.

————

It was several hours later that Kyle Dutton returned from the mainland. His boat had been washed ashore, and only after a terrible struggle had he succeeded in reaching a place where there were kindly hands to rescue him. With him came the physician he had gone to seek. The shadow of death that had hung over the lighthouse during that terrible night was lifted, and before many days the good dame was able to join in the rejoicing over the happiness that had come to Huldah Deane.

———————————

MRS. M. S. PETERS *wrote for popular magazines during the second half of the nineteenth century.*

NINETEEN

THE LUMINOUS WORLD
OF HELEN KELLER

Van Wyck Brooks

Nearing the end of the long story selection process for this book about heroes, the time came to review the stories I had decided to include, then search out heroes that should, under no condition, be left out. One of these must-include heroes was Helen Keller. The problem was that so much has been written about or by her that selecting the best story proved a daunting task. Finally I stumbled on this one penned by that great scholar and biographer, Van Wyck Brooks, and I knew I had found it at last.

When I was in St. Augustine, Florida, in the winter of 1932, Helen Keller appeared at the Cathedral Lyceum. I went to see and hear her there, drawn by curiosity such as one feels for any world-famous person. For Helen Keller had been famous from the age of ten, when she had sat on Edward Everett Hale's knee and Queen Victoria asked Phillips Brooks about her. Mark Twain had said that the two most interesting characters of the nineteenth century were, quite simply, Napoleon and Helen Keller. Yet there she was in St. Augustine, still young in 1932, and here she continues to be twenty-five years later.

I remember one phrase she uttered then, referring to the subway in New York that "opened its jaws like a great beast." I was not aware then how familiar she was, literally, with the jaws of beasts, for she had once stroked a lion's mouth. The lion, it is true, was young and well fed in advance, but nevertheless she entered its cage boldly; for her "teacher," as she always called Anne Sullivan, the extraordinary woman who developed her mind, wished her to meet experiences of every sort.

The daughter of a Confederate officer, Miss Keller was born on an Alabama farm and knew cows, mules, and horses from her earliest childhood; they had eaten apples from her hand and never harmed her; and her teacher, feeling that she should know wild animals as well, introduced her early to a circus zoo. She shook hands with a bear, she patted a leopard, she was lifted up to feel the ears of a giraffe. She encouraged elephants to wind their trunks about her neck and big snakes wrapped their coils about her. Helen Keller, for this reason partly, grew up without fear, and she has remained both physically and morally fearless.

The world in which Helen Keller lives is built of touch sensations, devoid of physical color and devoid of sound, and she has written much about the hand by which she lives and which takes the place of hearing and sight. She has "ten eyes for sculpture" the late professor Gaetano Salvemini said when, in 1950, she visited Florence and he arranged for her to see Michelangelo's Medici tombs and the sculpture of Donatello in the Bargello. Salvemini had movable scaffolds set up so that she could pass her hands over the Medici heads and St. John the Baptist, the figures of Night and Day, and the Madonna and Child. The sculptor Jo Davidson, who

was present, said he had never seen these sculptures as when he watched her hands wandering over the forms.

Exploring the faces of her friends and people whom she has just met, she reads them as if she were clairvoyant, and she can distinguish the Yankee twang and the southern drawl she has never heard by touching the throats of the speakers. She says that hands are quite as easy to recognize as faces and reveal the secrets of character more openly. In her land of darkness and silence she can feel with her own hands the beautiful, the strong, the weak, the comic. She can tell from hands whether people have large natures or whether they have only "dormouse valor."

Because two of her senses were cut off, nature augmented her three remaining senses, not the sense of touch alone but the sense of taste and the sense of smell. She tells in her *Journal* how in London, passing through a gate, she knew at once by the smell of burning leaves, with the smell of the grass, that she was in Green Park, and she says she can always distinguish Fifth Avenue from humbler New York streets by the odors issuing from the doors as she walks past. She knows the cosmetics that women are using and the kind of coffee they are roasting within and whether they use candles and burn soft coal or wood. "What lovely white lilacs!" she will exclaim, knowing they are white by touch or smell, for in texture and perfume white lilacs differ from purple.

Helen Keller, who cannot hear voices, feels vibrations. When an orchestra plays, she follows the music waves along the floor. Detecting on her desk upstairs the vibration of the pantry bell below, she answers with a shuffle of the feet, "Coming down!" "Listening" with her feet, she says, in a hotel dining room, she knows the moods and characters of people who walk past her, whether they are firm or indecisive, active or lazy, careless, timid, weary, angry or sad.

All this gave rise in early years to legends of a "wonder girl" that always annoyed Helen Keller—for she is the embodiment of humor and simple good sense. Anne Sullivan took pains to keep her from being a prodigy, but it was impossible to conceal the fact that she had a remarkable mind, and a still more remarkable will. Speaking of this, Emma Goldman said she proved that the human will had "an almost illimitable power."

Nothing could have been more tonic than Helen Keller's bringing up, under the guidance of Anne Sullivan, on the farm in Alabama. They read and studied out of doors on the riverbank, in the woods, in the fields, in the shade, as Helen remembered, of a wild tulip tree. The fragrance of the mimosa blossoms, the pine needles and the grapes were blended with all her early lessons. She learned about the sun and rain, and how birds build their nests, about squirrels, frogs, wildflowers, rabbits and insects; and, as it came back to her, everything that sang or bloomed, buzzed or hummed, was part of her education.

It was Anne Sullivan who had invented the methods of connecting mind with mind that made all this possible, of course—and that seemed to be "superhuman," as Einstein remarked.

What can one say of an intellect as handicapped as Helen's that carried her so far in so many directions? She early learned geography from maps that her teacher made out of river clay or sand, feeling mountains and valleys and following the courses of rivers. At the age of eighteen, if she had not mastered, she had learned much of geometry, algebra, physics, botany, zoology and philosophy. She wrote good letters in French; later she spoke German. She was reading Latin too when she went to college. Unable to hear lectures or take notes, she graduated with honors at Radcliffe, where she wrote her autobiography in the class of Charles Copeland, the famous

"Copey" who said she showed that she could write better, in some of her work, than any other man or woman he had had as a pupil.

Few of the required books were printed for the blind, and she had to have whole books spelled into her hand. Always examining, observing, reflecting, surrounded by darkness and silence, she wrote that she found music and brightness within. Through all her thoughts flashed what she supposed was color. With her native traits of pluck and courage, energy, tenacity, she was tough-minded and independent. She grew up fond of sports, riding a horse and a bicycle tandem, playing cards and chess and all but completely self-reliant.

In *Midstream*, she wrote that she had read her Braille Bible so often that in many places the dots had been rubbed off. "The Bible," she has said, "is the only book that reaches up to the times in which we live. It speaks knowingly of the sun, the skies, the sea and the beauty of distant stars."

Helen Keller has become a world citizen. She has toured six continents to help the blind. She has understood Japan and Greece and especially perhaps the Bible lands, where she has lectured at universities from Cairo to Jerusalem and where new schools for the blind have risen as she passed. Reaching out to meet the minds of all sorts and conditions of men, she comprehends their needs and aspirations.

Now it happens that, living myself in Connecticut, not far from Helen Keller, I have taken a few notes about her in recent years, jotting down chance remarks of hers and other memoranda, comments that from time to time she has suggested. I offer some of these, unconnected as they are:

July 1945: Helen has been out picking blueberries today. She has only to touch them to know when they are ripe.

The paths and garden at her house are all so perfectly kept that I exclaimed over them. Helen does it. In summer she is up at five every morning, edging the driveway and the paths, weeding the flower beds. (She distinguishes by touch between the flowers and the weeds.)

Dinner with Helen at Prof. Robert Pfeiffer's. Our Florentine hostess, Mrs. Pfeiffer, played an Italian song. Helen stood with her left hand on the piano, waving her right hand, keeping time. In this way she knows by heart Beethoven's *Ninth Symphony* and recognizes many other compositions.

Someone asked her how she tells the difference between day and night. "Oh," she said, "in the day the air is lighter, odors are lighter, and there is more motion and more vibration in the atmosphere. At night the air is dense and one feels less motion in things."

September 1945: We rode downtown in a bus to Grand Central Station. Helen likes to feel the crowd around her. Suddenly she said, "There is a painter in the bus." I looked around and, sure enough, there was a house painter at the other end of the bus, twenty feet away.

October 1949: Helen comes to dinner. One of our friends asked Helen how she had come to understand abstractions. She said she had found that good apples were sweet and that there were also bad apples that were bitter. Then she learned to think of the sweetness and bitterness apart from the apples as ideas in themselves.

December 1951: Usually Helen's typing is like an expert stenographer's, but the other day there were a few dim lines in one of her letters and she added this postscript: "Polly [Polly Thomson, Anne Sullivan's successor] says the writing of this machine doesn't please her critical eye. My apologies. H. K."

Polly likes to tease her, and she is sometimes severe with her. If Helen makes a mistake in typing, Polly makes her copy the page again. I must add what all their friends know, that Polly is in her way as extraordinary a person as Helen. Without her vitality and her diplomatic sense, what could Helen do in her journeys about the world? And what inexhaustible buoyancy both of them have! I have seen them together on a midnight train, when everyone else was asleep, smiling and chatting like birds on a branch in the morning.

June 1953: Helen is 73 years old today. This week she returned from a two months' absence in South America. What variety there is in her mind! She is interested in everything. She recalled to me the dancing of "La Argentina," though how she conceived of this so well I cannot imagine. And what happy phrases come to her mind! Some children spelled words into her hand and she said their small fingers were like "the wildflowers of conversation."

About Helen Keller, it seems to me, William James uttered the last word when he wrote, "The sum of it is that you are a *blessing*"—a verdict that has been ratified in hundreds of hospitals throughout the world where she has all but raised the dead. Someday the story will be told of the miracles she has performed, or what could have passed for miracles in less case-hardened ages, when the blind have opened inward eyes and really seen life for the first time after Helen Keller has walked and talked with them.

VAN WYCK BROOKS (1888–1963) *was one of America's greatest writers, biographers, essayists, and critics. Among his best-known books are* The Ordeal of Mark Twain *(1920),* The Pilgrimage of Henry James *(1925),* The Life of Emerson *(1932),* The Flowering of New England: 1815–1865 *(1936),* New England: Indian Summer, 1816–1915 *(1940),* Helen Keller, Sketch for a Portrait *(1956), and* Howells: His Life and World *(1959).*

THE ANSWER

Arthur Gordon

It all seemed so hopeless, and to fight against it akin to Sisyphus and his great rock: It would just *never* happen. Then his wife told him to go visit a convalescent in the hospital and to listen to his story. A story about a descendant of slaves who knew not the meaning of the word *impossible*.

———

The day had been long and hot. Some of us had spent most of it struggling with one of those civil rights problems that plague American towns from time to time. It had all been painfully familiar: the mayor listening in troubled silence; the surface politeness masking the deep grievances; the helpless feeling of having left the old simple right-or-wrong far behind and reaching the arid region where right clashes endlessly with right.

I came home tired and discouraged. "At times it seems hopeless," I said dejectedly to my wife. "The wounds are too old; the scar tissue is too thick. There just isn't any answer."

She was standing at the kitchen sink making a salad. "Oh, I

don't know," she said. "I heard a pretty good answer today. Down at the hospital."

(As a hospital volunteer, my wife pushes a cart full of magazines and paperbacks. She talks to patients, and patients talk to her. Sometimes, bored or lonely, they tell her all sorts of things about themselves.) In this case, she said, the editor of a small country newspaper was convalescing from an operation. She dried her hands on a dish towel.

"You ought to stop by and let him tell you the story he told me. I think you'd be impressed."

"Why can't you tell me what he said?" I asked.

"It wouldn't be the same. You ought to get it from him."

And so the next day I stopped by the hospital. The patient was still there, padding around in a dressing gown and slippers—a tall man with gentle blue eyes and a gift for words. We sat in the visitors' lounge, and this is the story he had to tell.

I was a timid six-year-old with braces on my legs, a frail, lost, lonely little boy when I first arrived at the farm in Georgia. Had it not been for an extraordinary woman, I might very well have remained that way.

She lived on the farm in a two-room cabin where her parents had been slaves. To an outsider she looked like any of the black people on the place, but to those who knew her she was a spiritual force whose influence was felt everywhere.

She was the first person called when there was sickness; she made medicines from roots and herbs that seemed to cure just about anything. She had a family of her own, but all of the children around felt that somehow they belonged to her. Her name reflected this. In the soft speech of the Georgia lowlands the word *maum* is a slurred version of *mama.* We called her Maum Jean.

Maum Jean talked to the Lord often and we all suspected that when she did, He stopped whatever He was doing, listened, and took appropriate action. Her heart reached out to small, helpless things, so she took particular interest in me from the start.

When I was stricken with polio at the age of three, I'm sure my parents didn't know what was the matter with me. All they knew was that times were hard and suddenly they had a crippled child on their hands. They took me to a New York City hospital, left me, and never came back. The people who took me into their foster home had relatives on the Georgia estate where I was sent in hopes that the warmer climate might help.

Maum Jean's sensitive emotional antenna instantly picked up the loneliness and withdrawal inside me, just as her marvelous diagnostic sense surveyed the polio damage and decided that, regardless of what the doctors might have said, something more ought to be done. Maum Jean had never heard the word *atrophy,* but she knew that muscles could waste away unless used. And so every night when her tasks were done she would come to my room and kneel beside my bed to massage my legs.

Sometimes, when I would cry out with pain, she would sing old songs or tell me stories. When her treatments were over, she would always talk earnestly to the Lord, explaining that she was doing what she could but that she would need help, and that when that day came she wanted Him to give her a sign.

A creek wound through the farm and Maum Jean, who had never heard of hydrotherapy, said there was strength in running water. She made her grandsons carry me down to a sandy bank where I could splash around pretty well.

Slowly I grew taller, but there was little change in my legs. I still used crutches; I still buckled on the clumsy braces. Night after night Maum Jean continued the massaging and praying. Then one morning, when I was about twelve, she told me she had a surprise for me.

She led me out into the yard and placed me with my back against an oak tree; I can feel the rough bark of it to this day. She took away my crutches and braces. She moved back a dozen paces and told me that the Lord had spoken to her in a dream. He had said that the time had come for me to walk. "So now," said Maum Jean, "I want you to walk over here to me."

My instant reaction was fear. I knew I couldn't walk unaided; I had tried. I shrank back against the solid support of the tree. Maum Jean continued to urge me.

I burst into tears. I begged. I pleaded. Her voice rose suddenly, no longer gentle and coaxing but full of power and command: "You can walk, boy! The Lord has spoken! Now walk over here."

She knelt down and held out her arms. And somehow, impelled by something stronger than fear, I took a faltering step, and another, and another, until I reached Maum Jean and fell into her arms, both of us weeping.

It was two more years before I could walk normally, but I never used the crutches again. For a while longer I lived in my twilight world, halfway between the whites, who considered me part alien, and the blacks, who could offer affection but no kinship. Then a circus came through town, and when it left, I left with it.

For the next few years I worked with one circus or another. Now and then, when the circus went into winter quarters, I would come back to the little town and help the editor of the weekly newspaper. There was little money in it, but I liked the smell of ink and the sounds of words. I never went back to the farm; a runaway seldom returns. But I always asked about Maum Jean, and when I could afford it I sent her little things.

Then the night came when one of Maum Jean's tall grandsons knocked on my door. It was late; there was frost in the air. Maum Jean was dying, he said, and she wanted to see me.

The old cabin was unchanged: floors of cypress, windows with wooden shutters—no glass, roof of palm thatch mixed with pitch. Maum Jean lay in bed surrounded by silent watchers, her frail body covered by a patchwork quilt. From a corner of the room, a kerosene lamp cast a dim saffron light. Her face was in shadow, but I heard her whisper my name. Someone put a chair close to the bed. I sat down and touched her hand.

For a long time I sat there. Around me the dark faces were grave and patient. There were no tears, no chants, all was quiet. Now and then Maum Jean spoke softly. Her mind was clear. She hoped I remembered the things she had taught me. Outside, the night wind stirred. In the other room the fire snapped, throwing orange sparks. There was a long silence; she lay with her eyes closed. Then the old voice spoke, stronger suddenly. "Oh," said Maum Jean with surprise and gladness, "it's so *beautiful!*" She gave a little contented sigh, and died.

And then something quite unbelievable happened: In the semidarkness her face seemed to glow. No one had touched the lamp. There was no other source of light. But her features, which had been almost invisible, could be seen plainly, and she was smiling. It lasted for perhaps ten seconds. It was most strange, but not at all frightening. I couldn't account for it then, and I can't account for it now. But I saw it. We all saw it. Then it faded and was gone...

My companion stopped speaking. In the corridor I heard the rattle of an instrument cart as a nurse hurried by. Finally he spoke again. "All that happened a long time ago. I live in another town now. But I still think of Maum Jean often, and the main thing she taught me: that nothing is a barrier when love is strong enough. Not age. Not race. Not anything."

I took a deep breath, remembering what my wife had said. The answer? Maybe someday. Someday…

ARTHUR GORDON (1912–   ) *still lives and writes from his natal seacoast of Savannah, Georgia. During his long and memorable career, he edited such magazines as* Cosmopolitan, Good Housekeeping, *and* Guideposts. *He is the author of a number of books, including* Reprisal *(1950),* Norman Vincent Peale: Minister to Millions *(1958),* A Touch of Wonder *(1983), and* Return to Wonder *(1996) as well as several hundred short stories.*

TWENTY-ONE

PLATTE RIVER RHAPSODY

Joseph Leininger Wheeler

The Platte River is born high in the mountains, in the snow that makes life possible for so many million people east of the Colorado Rockies. The Platte is only a trickle where its twins are born: one in the Mount Evans Wilderness and the other in the San Isabel National Forest. Many miles downriver they joyfully combine their waters. The Platte's youth is spent singing its rhapsody and gamboling down the deep ravines and canyons, towering mountains overhead, evergreens and aspens to the side. In flood season, everything in its way is battered down as though mere toothpicks—houses, bridges, and roads—it is no respecter of persons or things. Nothing can stand in its way. It is not tamed until it gets to the Front Range, until it slows down for its long ramble through east Colorado and Nebraska to its tryst with the Missouri River on the Iowa border.

Two's company, three's a crowd. Four—well, sometimes four can get along. And thus it was…oh…a number of years ago, with the three boys (Philip, Robert, and Andrew) and Tabby, the only girl. They were a foursome; they were neighbors on the road to Shadow Mountain; they were playmates. The neighbors laughingly called them "the Four Musketeers": all for one, one for all. They were the inseparables.

Tabby, though the youngest, ruled over the others as absolute autocrat. To preserve her sovereignty she was not ashamed to utilize every feminine wile that exists, and several that she apparently invented herself. Throughout their childhood games and play-acting, she took all the feminine parts: mother, wife, matriarch, queen; the three boys traded off the male roles.

Their favorite place to play was Uncle Henry's ranch. Extending nearly twenty-six hundred acres, it had everything children could desire: mountains, streams, caves, pines, firs, aspens, a century-old house, and several barns—and he had given them the run of it all. Though it was regularly the site of church picnics, youth group campouts, Kiwanis fund-raisers, and chamber of commerce activities, no one knew all the paths, streams, hideouts, and overlooks better than the four children.

All went well until puberty messed things up. One by one, each of them began to change, both externally and internally. Gone now was the peace of before. Gone was the willingness to trade roles with each other. Gone too was the all-for-one-and-one-for-all among the three boys, for now none of them wanted to share Tabby with another.

During the high school years Tabby, accepting dates from whomever of them asked her first, played no favorites. But deep down, it had always been clear that she was attracted to Philip most, Robert second, and Andrew least. Philip was the flamboyant one, the charismatic one, the adventurous one, the innovative one, the funniest one, the unpredictable one, the moodiest one, the

handsomest one, the most irresistible. Robert was the quiet one, the deepest one, the most intelligent one, the most sensitive one, the most empathetic one, the tenderest one, the dependable one, the most spiritual one, the only one of the three with a hyperactive conscience. Andrew was the wild card: Because he was insecure about who he was, he tended to be the follower, siding one time with Philip, one time with Robert; however, since Philip tended to dominate, more often than not Andrew sided with him, and when Tabby made her opinion felt, he invariably joined forces with her. Only rarely did Andrew take the lead in anything. He had one commendable trait, however: He was loyal. And once he had given his word, he could be depended upon to keep it. Tabby defied classification. Loving and sunny by nature, she was a born peacemaker and was chiefly responsible for the fact that the quartet quarreled so rarely. Of the four, hers was the quickest mind, moving with lightning speed, and hence her ascendancy over the others.

Over a period of several years, all four graduated from Evergreen High School and went on to the University of Colorado in Boulder. Philip majored in business. Robert majored in history; eventually he would go on to the Ph.D. Andrew majored in, well, whatever looked interesting at any given moment; in the end, just to get graduated, he settled for liberal arts. Then he joined a real estate firm, married a girl from his church, and had three children. Tabby specialized in theater and English, then earned a master's degree in English before she took a job teaching in her old high school. Her rich and throaty laugh with joy bells in it, and her ability to make everyone around her feel special, made her the center of attention wherever she might be. Not until her late twenties did she even consider getting serious about any of her many suitors; when she finally did, she surprised no one by settling on Philip and Robert as the two she spent the most time with. Robert, even though he'd known long before that in any showdown with Philip he'd end up the loser, pressed his suit anyhow.

And he was right in his premonition: Each day that passed it became ever more obvious that Philip had but to ask the question and it would be all over. Robert's heart sank, for always, for him, it had been Tabby and no other.

Then, one day, the terrible headline: BANK EMPLOYEE ACCUSED OF EMBEZZLING $240,000. And the employee was Philip. There followed a number of related headlines, gradually lapsing into mysterious silence, with Philip still not arrested and, strangest of all, remaining employed by the bank. The entire city of Denver was confused over the issue: Why wasn't he in jail? The bank president answered no questions on the matter but merely smiled and declared the matter settled: There was no longer a shortage.

But for Tabby it was not that simple. She had always maintained that she would never marry a man she didn't respect. Philip did not help at all, for whenever she questioned him on the matter he smoothly deflected it by saying, "The matter's been settled." Since Philip's father was one of the wealthiest men in Colorado, that evasive answer failed to solve Tabby's inner question: *Yes, but did you embezzle the money?*

————

Eight long months passed, and the tide of Tabby's love gradually shifted...back toward Robert. Nevertheless, Robert, even in the ecstasy of finally being first with Tabby, could not help but notice the difference between the fond looks she gave him and the passion in her eyes when she had looked at Philip. (William Butler Yeats would have described her thus: "when all the wild summer was in her gaze").[1] But when she looked at Robert, true there was tenderness in her eyes, true the flame of love flickered there, but it was as though the rheostat of her passion had been dimmed to 60 percent power. There were hidden lines of sadness beneath the surface of her unblemished cheeks. Robert was the only man in the world who would have caught it. She was not merely a piece of his world, she was *all* his world, and hence he knew her every expression: the nuances, the shades, even the quicksilver flickerings.

How heartbreaking to be loved less than another, to see the radiance of that beloved sun dim as though a cloud had passed in front of it and to know you were that cloud. But Robert also knew it was a miracle that she cared even this much for him—and he would gratefully accept it, even as a beggar accepts spare change. Not because it brought great joy to him but because the alternative was a total eclipse of the sun of her love.

Furthermore, he knew full well that he was first in her affections only because she'd lost all respect for Philip. In other words, she could be his only by default.

AUTUMN ALONG THE PLATTE

It was autumn on the north branch of the Platte. No longer swollen with snow from the high country, the river was now serene—almost, in fact, sedate. It was that magical time of the year when Indian summer lingers, reluctant to leave, and winter is too polite to intrude on another's protracted good-byes. Not even a wisp of a cloud marred the cerulean blue of the sky. Waves of evergreens undulated into infinity, the greens so varied that the effect was almost iridescent or impressionistic. Great monoliths of stone towered a thousand feet or more above the slumbering river. In the occasional still pools could be seen reflections of burnished gold— the time of the aspens had come.

Tabby leaned against a moss rock, a faraway look in her eyes, her body sinuous and uncharacteristically lazy, stretched out as a cat. She'd been born with that feline look, hence the nickname that long ago had obliterated all memory of her real name. Over time, as she'd matured into glorious womanhood, her catlike grace, beauty, and contours remained a constant. While not drop-dead beautiful, she had perfect skin that comes from a tobacco-free healthy lifestyle, long lustrous dark brown hair with bronze overtones, and an inner radiance that glowed through her eyes. Robert had tried many times to capture the totality but invariably came up short. The closest he'd ever come was this: *She has deep wells of kindness, empathy, unselfishness, caring, consideration, and spiritual faith to draw from; and she's so wondrously alive that her eyes dance with* joie de vivre. *Every day of her life is too short for all she wants to do and experience during its twenty-four hours.*

Robert, leaning against a giant cottonwood, drank in every inch of her, limned as she was against the heart-stopping splendor of the autumn day. Unutterable longing for her bubbled up from his heart and into his eyes, but stopped short of his lips, for he prosaically observed, "That picnic lunch you made for us was just perfect!"

"Thank you," she purred.

"Yes, I'm about as satisfied as a man can get…except for…"

"Except for *what?*" she shot back, her mood changing at blinding speed.

"Except that I'll never be truly satisfied until…uh…uh…until you're my wife." *There—after all the years—the words were said at last.*

"Well, what's keeping that from happening?" she retorted, with that roguish look he adored.

And that's how it all happened, how the dreams of Robert's

childhood, adolescence, youth, and manhood coalesced into a fairy-tale ending. He gathered into his starved arms all that had seemed impossible, all that still seemed but an illusion.

UNCLE HENRY'S LETTER

Henry Thompson was his name. However, most of the town knew him simply as "Uncle Henry," for, though a bachelor (his one love had died of pneumonia many years before), he had always loved children and young people. After his fiancée died he threw himself into volunteer work. Whether it be Sunday school, Scouts, or YMCA, he was always there to mentor, to bridge, to make a difference. Without question, he was the most beloved man in town.

For some unexplainable reason, even to him, he had remained especially close to the Four Musketeers. Often, in fact, he'd been the only adult invited along on their picnics, hikes, and fishing expeditions. All four respected, revered, admired, and loved him. But of them all, Robert was dearest to him.

Well, as fate would have it, about two weeks after Tabby accepted Robert's proposal, Uncle Henry was felled by a sudden heart attack. Robert, dropping by for his usual evening visit, found him slumped over in his beloved rocker, his spirit returned to his Maker.

In the whirlwind days that followed, it became increasingly clear that Uncle Henry had died almost bankrupt. This surprised everyone, for it had always been assumed that Uncle Henry was extremely wealthy. It turned out that even his great ranch and buildings were mortgaged to the hilt, with no equity left, and that only a few thousand dollars remained in his bank account.

After the funeral, held out-of-doors because virtually the entire town attended, Robert went back to the now-desolate house to pick up Uncle Henry's books and papers, which long ago had been promised to him. The bank president had told Robert, just the day before, "After the funeral, go ahead and pick up Uncle Henry's personal things. The ranch and everything remaining will be sold at auction anyway."

Inside the study were only a few hundred cherished books, some dog-eared old magazines, a photograph album or two, several stacks of letters (tied with violet ribbons), and a small box of personal papers. Idly Robert opened it and found, on the very top, a fat, sealed envelope with these words written on it: EXTREMELY CONFIDENTIAL. NOT TO BE OPENED UNTIL MY DEATH.

Not knowing what to expect, Robert opened the envelope, feeling as he did so that he somehow violated the sanctity that comes with death. The first words on the stationery jolted him, as they read, *To whom it may concern (or Robert Williams, who I suspect will see this first).*

Late afternoon shadows darkened the windows before he finished, for he had read each sheet a number of times, initially not believing his eyes, so out of character did certain sections appear for such a model of rectitude as Uncle Henry. This is how it began:

> I know this long letter will be a shock to whoever reads it
> first, but it just *had* to be written. In fact, I could not pos-
> sibly leave this brief life and face my Maker with this letter
> unwritten. Whoever that person may be—most likely Bob,
> as close and dear to me as a son—I ask of you the perhaps
> undeserved gift of kindness, and that you withhold judg-
> ment of me until you finish reading the entire letter.
>
> To fully understand all that I have to say it will be

necessary for me to time travel with you all the way back to my childhood. I was the younger of two children; my sister's name was Alice, and she was the light of my life. Only one year apart, we were *everything* to each other. Even more so after our parents were killed in a terrible train wreck when I was thirteen and Alice was fourteen. A crusty aunt agreed to take us in (since clearly no one else wanted us, it was her "Christian duty" to do it herself). She begrudgingly housed, clothed, and fed us until we had both completed high school. Then, only hours after my graduation ceremony, she called us into her sewing room and assaulted us with these unfeeling, icy words: "I've completed my task, the duty I owed your mother. But I'm done now, and you're on your own—so don't ever come back to me for *anything!* Now, go to your rooms and clear out your things. The $20 on your dresser will provide you with a start. No! No! No! No questions. Now GIT!"

Needless to say, we were a mighty forlorn twosome to be greeted so coldly only moments after the euphoria of graduation. But that was Aunt Gertrude: Never once had she so much as kissed or hugged either of us—she was stone cold, stem to stern.

Tough years followed. Make that *mighty tough!* In order to escape the dead-end situation in which Alice found herself—I, at least, had a job in a grocery store—in sheer desperation she accepted the first proposal that came her way. A greater mistake she never made in her life. Oh how I tried to dissuade her, for I knew the man well! I made all kinds of promises, offered to split every dollar I earned with her. All to no avail. She was too convinced that this man of her dreams would bring her a nice little house with a picket fence, a garden, pets, and children.

Her new husband turned out even worse than I had predicted. He was a drunkard, he was into drugs, and he violently beat her and the little boy who came along nine months later. Beat them with an almost satanic grin on his otherwise cold and heartless face. Alice stood this sadistic monster several terrible years, then fled with her battered little boy, leaving no forwarding address—not even for me. Years passed before I received a letter from her, but without an address, for she was still terrified that they would be tracked down. And it was several years later before I received another.

Well, one never-to-be-forgotten night, I got a call. It was from a nurse I had never met, and these were her words: "I'm your sister Alice's nurse, and I'm afraid my news isn't good. She's dying and needs you. I'd suggest you drop everything—and *hurry!*" Then she gave me directions.

I got there just in time. I hardly recognized that dissipated woman in the bed as my once-lovely and happy sister. In order to stay alive and take care of her son she'd become a woman of the streets. In this degenerate underworld she had also become hooked on heroin. Needless to say, her beauty and youth quickly vanished, and here she lay—an absolute wreck of a human being! I just stood there in a state of shock, bereft of speech. This was a tragedy beyond my wildest nightmares.

Much as I tried to hide it, she couldn't help noticing how horrified I was, and forestalled my first question: "No, I *couldn't* let you know where I was or *what* I was..." Then her ravaged face contorted and her voice became a wail. "Oh, Henry! I just couldn't let you see how deep into hell I'd sunk! And there's"—and here she coughed the first of many pneumonial coughs that told me she was on the very brink of eternity—"and there's very little time left for me, so listen, listen! [*cough! cough!*] and don't interrupt!"

In essence, what she told me was that her son Richard had descended into the same hell she had. He had been in and out of prison. In fact, she didn't have any idea where he was. More coughs followed, depleting what little reserves she had left. Finally, her voice now barely a whisper, she reached out her emaciated needle-scarred arm and clutched my wrist in almost a death grip. With each ragged word and wrenching cough costing her remaining lifeblood, she told me that yes, her son, Richard, was no good, a rotter, a criminal, but still he was her son, my only nephew, and a child of God. And she exacted from me a solemn vow (sworn on my belief in God and Holy Writ) that should Richard come to me for help—he had my address—because of the love I once held for her, I would provide that help. What else could I do? Deprive a dying woman of the only consolation she begged for? *Of course,* I promised. Almost the moment I did so, an ever-so-slight smile came to her lips, she tightened her grip on my wrist for an instant, there was a long sigh...and then the tragic story of her short life came to an end.

More years passed. Since I had no family of my own, I sort of adopted the young people of my town and tried to make a difference in each of their lives. Professionally, I did well, since I gave the job my all. Gradually I rose from the lowliest flunky to vice president of the bank, next in authority to the president himself. It was said that there was not a more honest man in the county than I. In fact, I took pride in that integrity for I had never knowingly compromised it.

Then Richard came into my life.

At first he only asked for small favors…"to help me get out of a bind," as he prefixed every request. As time passed, and he realized he could count on me when in trouble (his middle name) the amounts requested kept getting higher. And higher. He always had a good reason—many good reasons—and always, *this time,* he was going to begin paying me back. Oh, he was a wily con artist, knowing a soft touch and a good thing when he had it.

My investments went first; they were to have been my retirement. Next went my certificates of deposit and savings accounts. When all those assets were gone, then came liens on the ranch—until eventually the equity was gone too. By this time I was getting more than a little desperate and let Richard know that I no longer had any assets left. I know this all seems incredibly foolish, even stupid—I can hardly believe my own words, in fact, on this paper! But I had no family or heir to save for other than Richard, and I *had* made a solemn vow to help him whenever he asked for it. So what else could I do? And he always sounded so contrite, so sincere: "Just this *one* more time, Uncle Henry, and I'll make it! I'll be able to begin paying you back." So how could I know for certain that *this time* his promise might not turn out to be true?

After my admission that I had nothing left, Richard didn't contact me for a long time—several years, in fact. Relieved, I mistakenly assumed that this time (at long last!) he had turned his life around and made good. Then that terrible never-to-be-forgotten night! It was a dreary October evening and it had been spitting outside (rain, sleet, hail, snow alternating) for several days. I woke to the sound of thunderous knocking. Bleary-eyed, I stumbled to the door. And there stood Richard, soaked to the skin, looking terrified.

After coming in and drying out a bit, he rushed through his story. He *had* been going straight, he declared, and had stayed away from the old gang that had got him into so much trouble with the law. Until one day when they threatened to frame him if he didn't go along with them on a "gig" (that turned out to be a bank break-in). As it turned out, it was a frame-up anyhow. They robbed the safe of a little over $240,000 and fled with the money after locking Richard in the safe so he'd have to face the music alone. Nothing he could say in self-defense made any sense to the authorities. There he was, where the money had been.

Since the authorities doubted that they could squeeze much money out of him, and since they appeared more interested in recovering the money than in sending him to prison, they'd released him on bail. But if he didn't return with the money within a week, he'd be jailed and personally charged with the robbery. Richard ended his story by dropping down on his knees and pleading (tears streaming down his cheeks), "So, Uncle Henry, if you want to save me from being sent back to jail, you've just *got* to help me somehow! If you *don't* save me this one last time—take out a loan or something—I swear that I'll kill myself before I'll let myself get locked up for the rest of my life!"

So once again, good ol' Uncle Henry came through. Paid the ultimate price: my integrity. "Borrowed" $240,000 from the bank system by sleight-of-hand juggling of accounts. I had only one frail hope: Years before, I had loaned a close friend a large sum of money to help him buy a ten-thousand-acre ranch. Consequently, on paper at least, I had at least a quarter million in collateral, as the ranch had skyrocketed in value. If I could somehow persuade my friend to pay me off for $240,000, *quickly*, no one need ever know what I had done.

Alas! There was to be no happy ending. The very next morning, in front-page headlines, was a story about my friend declaring bankruptcy. Since he was apparently vastly overextended, I'd be lucky to ever get a few pennies to the dollar for the money I had loaned him. That was the darkest day of my life. For the first time, I felt my entire life to be an absolute failure. I was *ruined.* Oh, the money part meant little alongside the complete loss of my integrity. My reputation would be in shambles, and I would almost certainly spend the rest of my life behind bars,

So there I sat in the vault area of the bank, my head on the desk, sobbing. Since it was two hours after closing time, I thought I was alone, but I was wrong. Philip Talbot (a new teller and one of my most cherished friends) walked in on me. So complete had been my emotional breakdown that I felt I had no choice in the matter. I swore him to absolute secrecy, then told him the entire sad story.

When I finally finished, there was a long, long silence. Then he said, in a tone he'd never used before with me: "That was an *unbelievably stupid* thing you did, Uncle Henry! Your nephew's nothing but an unprincipled con man! Surely you must know that by now!"

I could only nod my head miserably.

There followed another long silence, broken only by

Philip's walking over to the window where he gazed unseeingly down the city street. Later, after what seemed like forever, he turned to me with a look of grim resolution on his face and warned me not to budge from the spot until he came back.

I aged years during the following forty minutes because I fully expected him to come back with company: the bank president and the police. Instead, he returned alone, slow of step and looking much older than when he'd left me. Knowing what I've learned since, I can see why. All he said, looking at me more kindly than before and placing his hand on my shoulder, was, "Uncle Henry, it's all taken care of."

"*What's* all taken care of?" I retorted in disbelief.

"Everything," he answered.

My mind refused to accept such a preposterous statement. I just stood there in unbelieving shock.

Then Philip continued, in the gravest, oldest voice I had ever heard him use: "But there *are* conditions, Uncle Henry."

"I *knew* it!" I muttered ungraciously.

He continued, as though he hadn't even heard me, "Yes, there are conditions—serious conditions. I have here with me a document that you must sign and date. I have the authority and license to notarize it. You will agree to the provisions in this document, swearing to the terms on your very faith in God and in His Holy Book."

I nodded dumbly.

Philip went on, his voice stern but with more than a trace of a sob in it. I now know why. "You *must* agree to carry this secret with you for life, sharing it with *no one.* I repeat: *for as long as you live and breathe.* Do you so promise?"

So out of it was I by this time, and so great was my feeling of relief at escaping with my honor intact, that I blindly accepted the terms. I do believe I'd have accepted *any* terms! Even the second part: that I should ask for early retirement from the bank effective January 1 of the following year (so as to not attract undue comment). Why this was required of me I could only guess. And none of the guesses were complimentary to me or to what I had done.

With a deep sigh, I signed, dated, and handed the document back to Philip.

He then looked me straight in the eye—and if ever in my life I've seen anguish in a man's eyes, I saw it then (but did not even guess what caused it). Then he exacted one further promise from me: that I would *never* ask him another question on the matter. I agreed, not knowing why he demanded such a promise of me. Two days later, I knew. The headline, *Bank Employee Accused of Embezzling $240,000,* said it all—even the supposed perpetrator's identity.

Yes, Philip had "confessed" to the crime…in order to save *my* reputation! I did not find out for a long time just how high a price he paid. Apparently he had borrowed the $240,000 on his own, from several different sources, refusing to ask his father for the money (fearing his father would either block him or give away the secret). Philip would pay it back over the years, out of his *own salary.*

All this the public never learned. Naturally, the story was the sensation of the year. However, when Philip was not taken to court, when the money was reported as "restored," the public gradually lost interest in the story. But, undeniably, there was something more than a little fishy about it.

That Philip's father was one of the bank's largest stockholders did little to rebuild the son's shattered reputation.

And there was no question but that Philip's reputation had taken a direct hit socially as well. As a result, he virtually disappeared from the social scene. Only with his three closest friends was he accepted—but not as he had been before.

The secret that took me the longest to learn—I did not break my vow—had to do with Tabby. I had thought Philip and Tabby as good as engaged. Couldn't help but see the love light in their eyes every time they looked at each other. Robert was courting her too, but deep down, I never felt he could win out over Philip. After the news broke, though, Tabby ceased to look at Philip with that radiance that comes only from mutual adoration between a man and a woman. Oh, she was polite, gentle, and caring with Philip, but it was not as before. One day I think she sensed my unarticulated question, and the words slipped out before she could stop them: "I could never marry a man I didn't deeply respect, Uncle Henry." When she belatedly realized what she had said, and their implications, she blushed ten shades of scarlet. But she did not retract the words.

That is when I knew the *real* price that Philip had paid on my behalf. And there was nothing I could do about it. *Ever!*

Recently, Tabby has been gravitating back to Robert. But bringing joy to Robert is not going to remove the perpetual sadness that ever haunts Philip's face.

Even Solomon in all his wisdom, faced with what has happened to three of the people I love most (as result of my unbelievably foolish act! I now realize that Richard will *never*

go straight!) would scratch his head. How in the world could
a mortal man untie such a Gordian knot? Only God
could—and even He would have to huff and puff a little.

There was more in the letter on other subjects, but to Robert
the letter stopped with that last sentence.

He returned home deeply troubled, determined to try to make
some sort of sense of this whole complex chain of events. He tossed
and turned, unable to sleep, all that interminable night. Next
morning he canceled every appointment he had, got into his Jeep,
and headed for the high country. Up and up he went, along the
serpentine road that ascends Upper Bear Creek Canyon. He did
not stop until he could see the white ramparts of Mount Evans
towering into the sky.

He got out, buckled on his canteen, and headed south, searching for a place of complete solitude. Finding a small, quiet clearing,
he spread his blanket and lay down, looking up into the deep blue
sky. What should he do? He really didn't have to do anything at all,
but that realization only made it much harder. All he had to do was
to do nothing and Tabby would remain his. After all, he had found
out only by chance. If someone else had found the letter first, he
might never have read the letter at all! *But,* snapped his conscience,
someone else didn't—you did! Clearly there would be no absolution
if he did nothing about what he had learned.

A great wave of love for Tabby thundered through his body.
How could he *possibly* give her up? Surely she'd learn to love him
more as the years went by. *Even if you do nothing about this letter?*
his conscience interrupted. *Will she not sense that there's something
big you're withholding from her?* He knew she would, for he knew
Tabby.

A shadow passed over him—a great eagle between him and infinity. That shadow layered itself in his mind. Would anything ever be the same—as simple—again?

He prayed, "Lord, please show me the way... I can't help thinking selfish thoughts, because I love Tabby so! You know how much I love her, Lord, for You know everything about me. But, Lord, how can I possibly face the long lonely years ahead *without her?*" Here moisture came to his eyes, and his words collided with each other and collapsed in an undecipherable heap. Some time later he resumed, "Lord, again I ask it—not my will, but Yours. What should I do?"

The sky turned saffron, rose, and crimson before the answer came. Although it was not the answer he had hoped for, it was the only one that offered peace. He must somehow, some way, find a way to get the truth and nobility of Philip's great sacrifice to Tabby—and without revealing that tightly woven tapestry of motivations, thoughts, words, and acts that had already cost so much heartbreak. After Tabby knew the truth at last, he would watch her face, her every expression, her body language, especially when Philip was in the vicinity. Then he would *know!*

After that, if what he suspected proved true, it would be up to *him* to break the engagement—for Tabby was too loyal, too inherently kind to ever go back on her word to him. But oh, how he hoped to be proven wrong: that her heart would remain his, even knowing the truth.

Later, he entrusted the matter to Andrew, after first swearing him to confidentiality. After hearing as much of the story as served the purpose, Andrew looked at him in disbelief.

"You're absolutely crazy, Bob! Why on God's green earth are you doing such a stupid, stupid thing? She's *yours* now. But if I tell her as much of the story as I can, without naming names, you will have sealed your doom. Without question, her heart will return to Phil."

"I know," sighed Robert miserably, "that's why it *must* be done—I could never live in peace with her unless I knew her heart was truly mine."

Andrew looked at him a long time in complete silence. Finally a look of deep respect came into his eyes. "All I can say, Bob, is…you're a better man than I. Were Tabby mine, *never* would I take such a risk of losing her."

Robert had no answer to give.

———————

It was over. Andrew told Tabby the truth, after swearing *her* to confidentiality. Before he'd even finished telling it, over her lovely face swept a sunrise of joy and relief. "I knew he couldn't have done such a thing!" she sang several times. That was followed, as the fuller implications of this new knowledge began to sink in, with a wrinkling of her creamy brow. How cruel she had been to Phil! How she had misjudged him—and yet he had never, by word or body language, defended himself. He had just taken it and sadly walked out of her life. What had she done?

———————

It didn't take Robert long to read the signs or feel the subtle withdrawal on her part when they were together—the slight lessening of her ardor for his embrace and kisses. Several times he surprised a faraway look in her eyes; each time she blushed and turned her eyes away.

Robert did what he knew he had to do: He broke off the

engagement. He told her that though he'd always love her, he just didn't feel ready for marriage yet. Perhaps he would later. Perhaps he was the type who couldn't handle being tied down to lifetime commitment. He was asking her to release him.

At first she avoided his eyes. Later he avoided *hers,* knowing that if their eyes met once more he could not possibly keep the truth from her—she would *know,* and all that he'd done to free her to follow her own heart would have been for naught. So his lame excuses sputtered to a halt. He stood up, hugged her without meeting her eyes, and walked away, his heart broken.

Philip and Tabby were married that following April. The intense love between the two was so apparent that many in the front rows found it necessary to reach for their handkerchiefs and wipe something out of their eyes. Andrew was best man. Robert was an usher; he would not agree to come closer to Tabby and Philip and the altar. Philip, not knowing why the engagement had been broken, didn't press the matter but felt there was more to the story than he'd been told.

That night Robert wept as he had never wept in his life—and never would again.

TWENTY YEARS LATER ON THE PLATTE

Philip and Andrew were fishing on their favorite river, now enlarged by late-spring runoff. For several months now, so heavy had been the winter's snowpack that the river had been running high and wide. That evening, relaxing by the crackling fire, Andrew leaned back and remarked blissfully, "Now *this* is livin'!"

Philip agreed.

After a time Andrew spoke again, "Some alumni weekend that was, huh?"

"Yep. All the old gang was there. All except for good ol' Bob."

"Oh, he's on sabbatical. Doing research on his next book in Edinburgh, Scotland. Some historical novel, I believe."

Philip was silent for a time, then said, sort of offhand, "Wonder why he never married."

Andrew didn't answer, but after a while he changed the subject: "How're things with you and Tabby? She…uh…looked sort of down at alumni—not her usually bubbly self."

This time it was Philip who didn't answer. Finally, when the silence was becoming embarrassing, he half laughed and said, "Guess I'd better tell you. Tabby and I'll probably split. I…uh… have met someone else."

He wasn't expecting the explosive response from Andrew, who leaped to his feet, anger darkening his face. "You can't, Phil, you can't—you just *can't!*" he spat out.

Now it was Philip's turn to get angry. "Oh yeah, I'd like to know what right *you* have to tell me how to run my life!"

All Andrew could say was, "You can't, Phil, you just can't!"

In near fury, Philip turned on him, his lip curling, and snarled out, "Give me one good reason!"

Without thinking, Andrew blurted, "Because…because the price paid for you was too high." Then he stopped, face blanching, and muttered in chagrin, "Never mind me, forget what I said. Don't know why I got so worked up."

But it was too late. Philip's face lost its anger and he looked long and hard at his friend. "That lame excuse won't wash, Andy. There's more to the story than that—in fact, I've *always* known there was more to the story. Come now, come clean. *Tell me!*"

Andrew sighed, "Guess I've done it now."

Philip icily agreed, not giving an inch. "Guess you have. I'm waiting."

"Well, I will, on one condition."

"*What* condition?"

"That you swear you'll *never* tell a soul—especially Tabby and…uh…Bob…as long as you live."

"And…*Bob?*"

"Yes."

"*All right.* I promise. *Now tell me!*"

So Andrew told him.

Afterward there was a long, long silence. Some time later it was Philip who broke it, and he didn't even sound like himself as he struggled for control. Finally he said, "And Bob did all that for *me?*"

"And Tabby."

"*Oh.*"

———

Next morning they returned home. Never again was there talk of "another woman."

———

AUTUMN RHAPSODY

Year after year, spring, summer, autumn, and winter sped by in the Colorado Rockies. Babies were born and became children, teens, adults. But no children ever came to Philip and Tabby. Not because they didn't want them. Both led busy lives: Philip was president of a consortium of banks, and Tabby taught English and theater in Conifer High School. Tabby had long since forgiven him, but not knowing what caused his sudden change of mind about divorcing her had driven a wedge into the marriage, a wedge that never went away. Once, when Robert's name was brought up, Philip quickly changed the subject and walked out of the house with a strange look on his face. Tabby wondered why Phil never wanted to talk about Bob any more. They had been such good friends; then suddenly, for some inexplicable reason, Bob ceased to drop by. In fact, it was painfully obvious that Phil no longer wanted him around. It hurt Tabby. It hurt even more that she could never explain to Bob why their door had been slammed in his face.

———

The high-pressure business world finally caught up with Philip. One evening, just before locking up for the day, he was felled by a massive stroke. The head teller phoned 911 first, then Tabby. Told her to come quickly.

She got to the hospital in record time. He lay there on a bed in the ER, her dear Phil, unable to move one side of his body, his face ashen. Their doctor stood at Phil's side, a grave look in his eyes. Tabby dropped down on her knees and tenderly held Philip's head to her breast, "Phil, Phil, Phil!" she whispered. "Wha...wha... what's happened?"

He tried to tell her but couldn't seem to get the words out. She turned to the doctor, who beckoned her to follow him into another room.

"Is...is...he going to be all right?"

The long silence that followed provided her answer. Finally the doctor answered, choosing his words carefully: "Anything is possible."

"But not probable?"

"But not probable."

———

A little over three weeks later, at 2:18 A.M., a call came from the doctor.

"Tabby?"

"Yes?"

"Sorry to wake you, but I think you'd better get back down to the hospital—*fast.*"

"I'll be there!"

About forty-five minutes later, she walked into the familiar hospital room. She had spent ten to twelve hours a day there ever since the stroke. Philip was awake and aware of her. He smiled and weakly reached out for her hand. He could speak! True, his words slurred, but she could still understand him. In her joy at this, she overestimated his improvement. He was the one to bring her back to earth.

"Tabby?"

"Yes, dear?"

"I...uh...don't have much...time left."

"O-o-o-o-h!"

"Please, let me talk while I...still can. I...uh...can't go...without...telling you."

Slowly, haltingly, he told her what Andrew had revealed that day on the Platte. Told her the whole story, in halting words. It seemed to take forever to tell. At the end, in a pleading tone so unlike him, Philip said, "Tabby, please forgive me."

"For what?"

"Because...I didn't want Bob...around anymore."

"Why not?"

"Because he...still loves you. Always *has* loved you."

————

Another year had passed. The snows had blanketed Philip's tombstone all winter. Then came spring with dandelions and lupines; summer with Indian paintbrushes and columbines; and now that it was autumn the aspens were bidding their fiery adieus in umber, orange, yellow, and green.

And once again, on the North Platte, the river rolled on, still singing its rhapsody but more serenely now. Up the bank at a turn of the river, outside a rustic cabin of great beauty, a man sat on a bench under a towering Ponderosa pine. He was a distinguished-looking man, with hair of silver gray. Virile, self-confident, at peace with himself. He held a book in his hands, but he was not reading it. His thoughts swirled back in time, back to a time when his world was golden like this day of heart-stopping beauty, back when life and love and overpowering joy were still possible. Yes, he was dreaming. Dreaming of Tabby. All his life—morning, noon, evening, and night—she was the stuff his daydreams and night dreams were made of. How often in recent years had he looked up from his bench and seen her standing there, wearing clothing that matched the season. Some nights she would walk on the moon's silver path across the shimmering river, coming slowly up to him in a filmy gown, luminescent and ethereal. But each time, after his longing arms reached out to her, she dissolved and he was left with only the singing river as company. As the long, lonely years passed, more and more he lived in the past, for that was where he found Tabby.

His mind fast-forwarded to Philip's funeral—and Tabby, her eyes red from weeping, but standing like Guinevere to thank those who had come. He had signed the register but could not bring himself to speak to her. It had been so long since he had felt welcome in their home. Why the sudden chill had caused Philip to shut him out, he had no idea. It had all happened so quickly: One day he was welcome as always, the next day he was not. Because of this, Robert had not known what to say to Tabby at the church. And now it was too late to say whatever those words might have been.

A slight noise, a rustling, startled him. He looked up.

At first, deeming it merely another of her dream appearances, he just sat there with a seraphic smile on his face, taking her in: still lovely, still feline, but the years had etched their path across her face. He was reminded of Shakespeare's description of Cleopatra:

> Age cannot wither her, nor custom stale
> Her infinite variety; other women cloy
> The appetites they feed, but she makes hungry
> Where most she satisfies.[2]

Suddenly, his book dropped to the ground as the apparition continued to look tenderly at him. *Why, this was no dream—this was real!* It was the eyes that proved her reality, for never in his dreaming had he seen them close up. Eyes that blazed a love for him he'd never seen there before, the intensity almost blinding him. He had not believed it possible that Yeats's "all the wild summer" look could ever come back, but here it was!

He could only struggle to his feet and sputter inanely. "So...you know?"

She smiled. "Yes, Phil told me...at the very end."

Robert was old, but not too old to know when he was due back on the center stage of life, back on stage as the hero this time, not the understudy.

The lines...oh, the blessed lines...came to him.

Why should they not? He'd been rehearsing them all his life.

---

1. From Yeats's poem, "The Folly of Being Comforted," included in *Poems of Today,* 1915.
2. *Anthony and Cleopatra,* William Shakespeare, act 3, scene 2.

ACKNOWLEDGMENTS

Introduction: "On the Trail of a Hero," by Joseph Leininger Wheeler. Copyright 2001. Printed by permission of the author.

"Heroes of Today," by Ruth Lees Olson. Published in *The Youth's Instructor,* March 6, 1934. Reprinted by permission of Joe Wheeler (P.O. Box 1246, Conifer, CO 80433) and Review and Herald Publishing Association, Hagerstown, Maryland.

"One Suffering One," by Arthur A. Milward. Published in *Insight's Most Unforgettable Stories,* 1990, Review and Herald Publishing Association. Reprinted by permission of the author.

"God's Eager Fool," by John A. O'Brien. Reprinted by permission from *Reader's Digest,* March 1946. Copyright © 1946 by The Reader's Digest Association, Inc.

"Aunt Becky's Boys," by Carrie B. Ilsey. Published in *The Youth's Instructor,* March 20, 1928. Reprinted by permission of Joe Wheeler (P.O. Box 1246, Conifer, CO 80433) and Review and Herald Publishing Association, Hagerstown, Maryland.

"He Knew Lincoln," by Ninde Harris. Published in *The Youth's Instructor,* February 3, 1931. Reprinted by permission of Joe Wheeler (P.O. Box 1246, Conifer, CO 80433) and Review and Herald Publishing Association, Hagerstown, Maryland.

"Germ-Proof," by Allison Ind. Published in *The Young People's Weekly,* November 4, 1933. Reprinted by permission of Joe Wheeler (P.O. Box 1246, Conifer, CO 80433) and David C. Cook Ministries, Colorado Springs, Colorado.

"The Bird Man," by Mary Brownly. Published in *The Youth's Instructor,* March 10, 1925. Reprinted by permission of Joe Wheeler (P.O. Box 1246, Conifer, CO 80433) and Review and Herald Publishing Association, Hagerstown, Maryland.

"Hero in Feathers," by Ella A. Duncan. Published in *The Youth's Instructor,* November 1, 1949. Reprinted by permission of Joe Wheeler (P.O. Box 1246, Conifer, CO 80433) and Review and Herald Publishing Association, Hagerstown, Maryland.

"A New Celebration of Memorial Day," by Margaret W. Beardsley. Originally published in *Wellspring,* date unknown. This text was published in *The Youth's Instructor,* May 25, 1926. Reprinted by permission of Joe Wheeler (P.O. Box 1246, Conifer, CO 80433) and Review and Herald Publishing Association, Hagerstown, Maryland.

"Coals of Fire," author unknown. If anyone can provide knowledge of authorship, earliest publication date, and publisher of this old story, please relay that information to Joe Wheeler (P.O. Box 1246, Conifer, CO 80433).

"A Place in the Sun," by Martha F. Simmonds. Published in *The Young People's Weekly,* May 26, 1934. Reprinted by permission of Joe Wheeler (P.O. Box 1246, Conifer, CO 80433) and David C. Cook Ministries, Colorado Springs, Colorado.

"A Girl Against a Blizzard," by Helen Rezatto. Reprinted with permission from the *Reader's Digest,* March 1962. Copyright © 1962 by The Reader's Digest Association, Inc.

"The Radio Notwithstanding," by G. E. Wallace. Published in *The Youth's Instructor,* November 22, 1938. Reprinted by permission of Joe Wheeler (P.O. Box 1246, Conifer, CO 80433) and Review and Herald Publishing Association, Hagerstown, Maryland.

"The Way of the Cross," by Margaret E. Sangster Jr. Published in *The Young People's Weekly,* April 1, 1933. Reprinted by permission of Joe Wheeler (P.O. Box 1246, Conifer, CO 80433) and David C. Cook Ministries, Colorado Springs, Colorado.

"A Matter of Honor," by William T. McElroy. Published in *The Youth's Instructor,* July 23, 1929. Reprinted by permission of Joe Wheeler (P.O. Box 1246, Conifer, CO 80433) and Review and Herald Publishing Association, Hagerstown, Maryland.

"Crumpled Wings," by John Scott Douglas. Published in *The Young People's Weekly,* January 9, 1932. Reprinted by permission of Joe Wheeler (P.O. Box 1246, Conifer, CO 80433) and David C. Cook Ministries, Colorado Springs, Colorado.

"War on Yellow Fever," by Ruth Fox. If anyone can provide knowledge of earliest publication date and publisher of this old story, please relay that information to Joe Wheeler (P.O. Box 1246, Conifer, CO 80433).

"Huldah Deane's Heroism," by Mrs. M. S. Peters. Published in *Harper's Young People,* May 2, 1882.

"The Luminous World of Helen Keller," by Van Wyck Brooks. Condensed from *Helen Keller: Sketch for a Portrait,* copyright © 1954, 1956. Used by permission of Dutton, a division of Penguin Putnam, Inc. It also appeared in *Reader's Digest,* August 1954. Used by permission of The Reader's Digest Association, Inc.

"The Answer," by Arthur Gordon. Published in Gordon's *A Touch of Wonder* (Old Tappan, N.J.: Revell, 1974). Reprinted by permission of the author.

"Platte River Rhapsody," by Joseph Leininger Wheeler. Copyright © 2001. Printed by permission of the author.